CONTENTS

Welcome to *100 Task Cards: Figurative Language*

Reading comprehension is more critical now than ever. Today's students are expected to navigate a wide variety of texts in order to succeed at reading, writing, test-taking, and more. If a news story features the idiom *a wolf in sheep's clothing* or a fiction tale contains the hyperbolic statement "I hit the ceiling," kids will need a clear understanding of figurative language to glean the essential meaning of the text.

Figurative language is defined as *language that means something other than what the words actually say*. This shape-shifting literary device can take many forms, including idioms, similes, personification, hyperbole, and irony. That makes it extra tricky to grasp—especially for the many ELL and ESL students who are in the process of cracking the code of a brand-new language.

But don't despair. This practical resource is here to help every child recognize and master this varied literary device in just minutes a day! The 100 task cards in this book offer motivating mini-passages with key questions related to:

- **Idioms**
- **Similes**
- **Metaphors**
- **Personification**
- **Hyperbole**
- **Understatement**
- **Irony**
- **Onomatopoeia**
- **Alliteration**

The cards are designed for instant use—just photocopy them and cut them apart, and they're good to go. The cards are also designed for flexible use. They're perfect for seatwork, centers, or meaningful homework. They're great for independent practice or work with partners, small groups, and even the whole class.

The questions on the cards will help students hone critical comprehension skills they'll rely on for a lifetime. And here's more good news: Because the mini-passages were written by professional authors with a gift for engaging young readers, kids will absolutely *love* them!

So what are you waiting for? Read on for tips that will help your students grow into confident, fluent, "deep" readers—quickly and painlessly. And don't forget to look for the other great *100 Task Cards* books in this series, including: *Informational Text, Literary Text, Text Evidence, Making Inferences,* and *Context Clues.* The kids in your class will thank you.

About the 100 Figurative Language Task Cards

This book contains 100 cards, each with a mini-passage. The stories vary by topic and tone in an effort to give students a rich variety of reading material that correlates with current state standards. (For a list of the standards these cards address, see page 8.) Each card presents five key questions, including at least three directly related to figurative language. Each card also includes a context clue. This special feature is intended to boost your students' abilities to glean the meaning of unfamiliar words they encounter in all texts.

The cards address the following specific categories of figurative language: idioms, similes, metaphors, personification, hyperbole, understatement, irony, onomatopoeia, and alliteration. The mini-passages can be used in any order you choose. However, if you are teaching a certain topic or wish to help students hone a particular skill—such as interpreting idioms—you can simply assign one or more cards from that category.

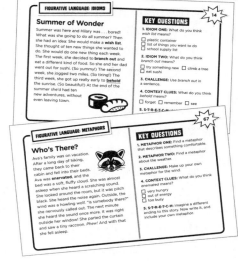

SAMPLE CARD: Here's a quick tour of a task card.

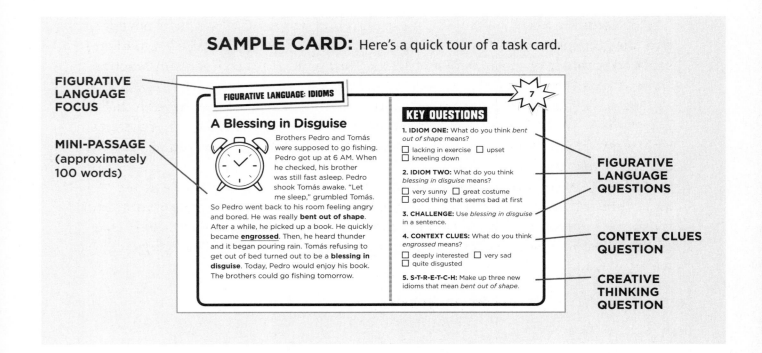

FIGURATIVE LANGUAGE FOCUS

MINI-PASSAGE (approximately 100 words)

FIGURATIVE LANGUAGE: IDIOMS

A Blessing in Disguise

Brothers Pedro and Tomás were supposed to go fishing. Pedro got up at 6 AM. When he checked, his brother was still fast asleep. Pedro shook Tomás awake. "Let me sleep," grumbled Tomás. So Pedro went back to his room feeling angry and bored. He was really **bent out of shape**. After a while, he picked up a book. He quickly became **engrossed**. Then, he heard thunder and it began pouring rain. Tomás refusing to get out of bed turned out to be a **blessing in disguise**. Today, Pedro would enjoy his book. The brothers could go fishing tomorrow.

KEY QUESTIONS

1. **IDIOM ONE:** What do you think *bent out of shape* means?
   - ☐ lacking in exercise ☐ upset
   - ☐ kneeling down

2. **IDIOM TWO:** What do you think *blessing in disguise* means?
   - ☐ very sunny ☐ great costume
   - ☐ good thing that seems bad at first

3. **CHALLENGE:** Use *blessing in disguise* in a sentence.

4. **CONTEXT CLUES:** What do you think *engrossed* means?
   - ☐ deeply interested ☐ very sad
   - ☐ quite disgusted

5. **S-T-R-E-T-C-H:** Make up three new idioms that mean *bent out of shape*.

FIGURATIVE LANGUAGE QUESTIONS

CONTEXT CLUES QUESTION

CREATIVE THINKING QUESTION

About the 14 Comprehension Helper Cards

To scaffold student learning, we've provided 14 Comprehension Helper cards on topics ranging from idioms to onomatopoeia. (See pages 9–15.) These "bonus" cards are intended to provide grade-perfect background information that will help students respond knowledgeably to the five questions on each of the 100 task cards. We suggest you photocopy a set for each student to have at the ready.

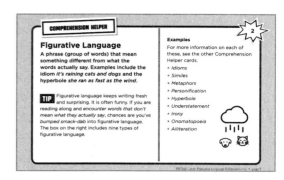

About the Answer Key

We've also included a complete answer key. (See pages 67–80.) In the key, we've provided sample responses to the questions on all 100 cards. Please note that some answers will vary. Because many of the questions are open-ended and no two minds work exactly alike, we encourage you to accept all reasonable answers.

MAKING THE TASK CARDS

The task cards are easy to make. Just photocopy the pages and cut along the dashed lines.

- **Tip #1:** For sturdier cards, photocopy the pages onto card stock and/or laminate them.

- **Tip #2:** To make the cards extra appealing, use different colors of paper or card stock for each category.

- **Tip #3:** To store the cards, use a plastic lunch bag or a recipe box. Or, hole-punch the corner of each card and place them on a key ring.

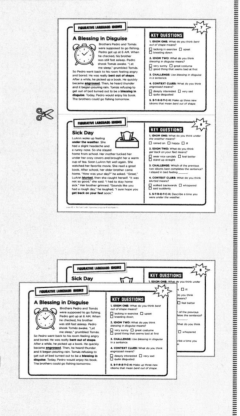

First-Time Teaching Routine

Any text will become accessible to students who bring strong reading strategies to the table. Here's an easy routine for introducing the task cards to your students for the very first time.

1. Discuss and review the featured figurative language topic. **TIP:** Share some or all of the Comprehension Helper cards on pages 9–15.

2. Display an enlarged version of a task card, using an interactive whiteboard, document camera, or overhead projector.

3. Cover the mini-passage and display just the title. Read it aloud and invite students to predict what the nonfiction story will be about.

4. Read the mini-passage aloud, slowly and clearly.

5. Boost fluency by inviting a student volunteer to read the mini-passage again, using his or her best performance voice.

6. Discuss the mini-passage. Encourage students to comment and connect it to other articles and books they've read as well as to their own lives.

7. Call attention to the five key questions to the right of the mini-passage. Model how to properly explore the featured phrases and surrounding text to unlock meaning. **TIP:** Use a highlighter to mark clues in the passage.

8. Challenge students to respond thoughtfully to each question.

9. Number and record each answer on chart paper. Model using complete sentences with proper spelling and punctuation.

10. Give your class a round of applause for successfully completing a task card. Now they're ready to tackle the cards independently.

INTEGRATING THE TASK CARDS INTO THE CLASSROOM

The task cards can be used in many ways. Here are 10 quick ideas to maximize learning:

- Challenge students to complete one task card every morning.

- Invite partners to read the task cards together and respond in writing.

- Ask small groups to read, discuss, and respond to the task cards orally.

- Place the task cards in a learning center for students to complete independently.

- Carve out time to do a task card with the whole class a few times a week.

- Encourage individual students to build fluency by reading a task card aloud to the class. They can then solicit answers from fellow students.

- Laminate the task cards and place them in a recipe box for students to do after they've completed the rest of their work.

- Send the task cards home for students to complete, with or without parental help.

- Provide students with designated notebooks for recording the answers to all of the task cards.

- Create a class chart, telling students to make a check mark each time they complete a task card. The first student to reach 100 wins a prize!

The lessons in this book support the College and Career Readiness Anchor Standards for Reading in Grades K–12. These broad standards, which serve as the basis for many state standards, were developed to establish rigorous educational expectations with the goal of providing students nationwide with a quality education that prepares them for college and careers.

Key Ideas and Details

- Refer to details and examples in a text when explaining what the text says explicitly and when drawing inferences from the text.

- Determine a theme of a story, drama, or poem from details in the text; summarize the text.

- Describe in depth a character, setting, or event in a story or drama, drawing on specific details in the text (e.g., a character's thoughts, words, or actions).

- Quote accurately from a text when explaining what the text says explicitly and when drawing inferences from the text.

- Cite textual evidence to support analysis of what the text says explicitly as well as inferences drawn from the text.

- Describe how the plot of a particular story or drama unfolds in a series of episodes as well as how the characters respond or change as the plot moves toward a resolution.

Craft and Structure

- Determine the meaning of words and phrases as they are used in a text, including those that allude to significant characters found in mythology (e.g., *herculean,* as related to Hercules).

- Compare and contrast the points of view from which different stories are narrated, including the difference between first- and third-person narrations.

- Compare and contrast two or more characters, settings, or events in a story or drama, drawing on specific details in the text (e.g., how characters interact).

- Describe how a narrator's or speaker's point of view influences how events are described.

- Explain how an author develops the point of view of the narrator or speaker in a text.

- Analyze how a particular sentence, chapter, scene, or stanza fits into the overall structure of a text and contributes to the development of the theme, setting, or plot.

Integration of Knowledge and Ideas

- Compare and contrast the treatment of similar themes and topics (e.g., opposition of good and evil) and patterns of events (e.g., the quest) in stories, myths, and traditional literature from different cultures.

Source: © Copyright 2010 National Governors Association Center for Best Practices and Council of Chief State School Officers. All rights reserved.

Literary Text

A piece of writing, such as a story or poem, that has the purpose of telling a tale or entertaining.

TIP *Before reading*, look at the title. What do you think the story will be about? *During reading*, stop and make predictions about what will happen next. Reread the parts you especially like or find confusing. *After reading*, reflect on the story. Compare it to other books and movies as well as your own life. Ask yourself, "What did the author want to tell me? What did I learn?"

Examples

- *Fantasy*
- *Science Fiction*
- *Thrillers*
- *Legends*
- *Folktales*
- *Tall Tales*
- *Horror*
- *Romance*
- *Tragedy*
- *Adventure*
- *Friendship*
- *Realistic Fiction*
- *Mysteries*
- *Comedies*
- *Fairy Tales*
- *Fables*
- *Drama*
- *Poems*
- *Short Stories*
- *Plays*

Figurative Language

A phrase (group of words) that mean something different from what the words actually say. Examples include the idiom *it's raining cats and dogs* and the hyperbole *she ran as fast as the wind*.

TIP Figurative language keeps writing fresh and surprising. It is often funny. If you are reading along and *encounter words that don't mean what they actually say*, chances are you've *bumped smack-dab* into figurative language. The box on the right includes nine types of figurative language.

Examples

For more information on each of these, see the other Comprehension Helper cards.

- *Idioms*
- *Similes*
- *Metaphors*
- *Personification*
- *Hyperbole*
- *Understatement*
- *Irony*
- *Onomatopoeia*
- *Alliteration*

COMPREHENSION HELPER

Idioms

A famous, commonly used phrase that means something different from what the words actually say. Idioms can be metaphors, such as *bored to tears*, or similes, such as *strong as an ox*. (See more examples at right.)

TIP Like popular online videos, idioms go "viral" because they are memorable. Idioms can relate to feelings, animals, colors, foods, weather, clothing, objects, sports, and more.

Examples
- *Bored to tears*
- *A sight for sore eyes*
- *Dull as dishwater*
- *Two peas in a pod*
- *Under the weather*
- *Shaking in his boots*
- *Put her foot in her mouth*
- *A slam-dunk*
- *Green with envy*
- *Hungry as a wolf*
- *Up in the air*
- *Like giving candy to a baby*
- *Sick as a dog*

COMPREHENSION HELPER

Similes

A descriptive phrase comparing two things using the words *like* or *as*, such as *blue <u>like</u> the sea* or *prickly <u>as</u> a cactus*. Good similes ring true and conjure images in people's minds. (See more examples at right.)

TIP Is *snug as a bug* a simile or a metaphor? To tell the difference between these two figures of speech, look for the word *like* or *as*. If one of them is present in the phrase, you've encountered a simile!

Examples
- *Sleep like a log*
- *Brave as a lion*
- *Like a rolling stone*
- *Right as rain*
- *Eat like a bear*
- *Tough as nails*
- *Like watching paint dry*
- *Cool as a cucumber*
- *Fits like a glove*
- *Sweet as sugar*

Metaphors

A descriptive phase comparing two things that does NOT use the words *like* or *as*, such as *he is a shining star* or *the lake was a silver mirror*. (See more examples at right.)

TIP Metaphors paint pictures in readers' minds. They can be short, such as *her eyes were jewels*, or long, such as *the storm clouds were rough, gray, looming tufts of steel wool*.

Examples

- *Her mouth is a rosebud.*
- *It's raining buckets.*
- *I'm a worn-out sail.*
- *Lynne is a night owl.*
- *Jamal is an early bird.*
- *The mall was a zoo.*
- *The sun is a shiny diamond.*
- *His backpack is a black hole.*
- *My brain is Swiss cheese today.*
- *The snow is a white blanket.*

Personification

Giving human characteristics to animals, objects, or ideas. Personification makes writing surprising and exciting. Examples include *the cat sighed, the flower bowed its head,* and *the correct answer raced out of her mind*. (See more examples at right.)

TIP To tell if a phrase contains personification, ask yourself two questions: 1. Is the thing being described NOT a person? 2. Is the thing being described treated as if it WERE a person? If you answer *yes* to both questions, you've encountered personification. *The girl whispered* is not personification but *the wind whispered* is!

Examples

- *The skyscraper kissed the sky.*
- *Two gray squirrels gossiped.*
- *The moon played hide and seek.*
- *A grasshopper sang at dusk.*
- *The tall grass shimmied.*
- *My dog hid his face in shame.*
- *A red motorcycle fled away.*
- *The stars winked knowingly.*
- *Joy danced in his brain.*

COMPREHENSION HELPER

Hyperbole

Exaggerated statements to make a point or add humor to a story. Examples include a *smile a mile wide* or a *line as slow as molasses*. (See more examples at right.)

TIP Think of hyperbole as stretching the truth—a lot!—for entertainment value. Sentences with hyperbole often end with an exclamation point for emphasis. To tell if a phrase is hyperbole, ask yourself two questions: 1. Is the statement *literally* true? 2. Could I imagine this statement in a tall tale? If you answer *no* to the first question and *yes* to the second, you've probably stumbled upon hyperbole.

Examples

- *She ran as fast as the wind.*
- *He was hungry enough to eat a horse!*
- *The man is as tall as a mountain.*
- *These shoes are killing me!*
- *Well, knock me over with a feather!*
- *This restaurant has been around since the Stone Age.*
- *My new dress cost a zillion dollars!*
- *I read the book a thousand times.*

COMPREHENSION HELPER

Understatement

Describing something as smaller, less, or worse than it actually is for dramatic effect. This figure of speech is used in writing and conversation to play it cool or to avoid boasting or making a fuss. Examples include: *I reckon 10 degrees below zero is a tad cold* and *Yes, I won the National Spelling Bee, but it is really no big deal.* (See more examples at right.)

TIP Understatement is the flip side of hyperbole: Instead of bragging, such as *I'm the fastest runner in the world!*, this figure of speech UN-brags, such as *I guess I'm not that slow.*

Examples

- *The desert is rather sandy.*
- *The ocean is kind of wet.*
- *Mount Everest is a little tall.*
- *That jalapeño pepper is a teensy bit hot.*
- *"I got a 100 on the test, which I guess is okay," she said.*
- *"The score of the soccer game was 10 to 0. We won by a hair," he said.*
- *"The richest person in the world has a bit of cash," he said.*

Irony

When words are used to convey the opposite of what those words literally mean. It is ironic when a boy falls in a mud puddle, then says, *I guess today was my lucky day*. It is also ironic when a girl sleeps until noon and her mother greets her by saying, *My, aren't you an early riser!* (See more examples at right.)

TIP Writers use irony to surprise readers and make them laugh. Unlike *understatement* which downplays reality, *irony* presents the opposite of reality. *Ten degrees below zero isn't too chilly* is understatement. *Ten degrees below zero is sweet, summer weather* is irony.

Examples

- *When a boy takes out the garbage and says, "Wow, this smells divine."*
- *When a girl with messy hair says, "Don't you love my fancy hairdo?"*
- *When a man spills his coffee and grumbles, "Awesome! That is just what I needed."*
- *When a woman is late for a meeting and announces, "I'm nothing if not punctual."*
- *When a caveman grunts, "They say I'm very modern and cutting-edge."*

Onomatopoeia

"Noisy" words that suggest the sounds that they describe: *Splat, burp, ring-a-ling.* (See more examples at right.)

TIP Onomatopoeia is often used in poetry and comics to bring exciting scenes to life. These words are often capitalized (BANG) or italicized (*whoosh*), or they end with an exclamation mark for emphasis (Zing!).

Examples

- *growl*
- *RUMBLE*
- *Crinkle*
- *whiff*
- *BOING*
- *oink*
- *Achoo!*
- *Zip*
- *Clap*
- *buzz*
- *CLANK*
- *snap*
- *crackle*
- *pop!*
- *MEOW*
- *rat-a-tat!*

COMPREHENSION HELPER

Alliteration

When several words in a phrase begin with the same sound. These words don't have to be right next to each other or even start with the same letter such as: *The cute, curious kitten can keep cool under the coconut tree.* (See more examples at right.)

TIP Alliteration makes writing more musical and exciting. Which sentence holds your interest more? 1. *The whale swam in the sea.* 2. *The white whale went swimming in the wonderfully rough seas of the West.* Bet you picked number two, due to its engaging alliteration.

Examples

- *big, bad, brown bear*
- *seven super-silly seals*
- *that goofy girl with the great big grin*
- *a boy named Buck, who blubbered like a baby*
- *marvelous mountains of Montana*
- *cool, colorful canyons of Colorado*
- *Please put the perfect pancakes on my pink-colored plate!*
- *The wind whooshed as I wandered through the woods.*

COMPREHENSION HELPER

Context Clues

Hints readers use to figure out the meaning of an unknown word in a text. Context clues can come before or after the unknown word.

TIP Authors use many words you may not know. But nearby words, phrases, and sentences can offer important clues to the definition of an unfamiliar word. As you read, play detective and search for clues to the mystery word's meaning. This will help improve your understanding and vocabulary without your having to reach for a dictionary.

Examples

- **Definition Clues:** *The unknown word is defined in the text.*
- **Example Clues:** *An example of the unknown word is provided in the text.*
- **Synonym Clues:** *A word with a similar meaning is near the unknown word.*
- **Antonym Clues:** *A word with the opposite meaning is near the unknown word.*

COMPREHENSION HELPER

Inference

Drawing a conclusion about a story based on clues in the text and your own background knowledge.

TIP To make an inference, hunt for "story clues" including how characters act and what they say. Think about similar books and movies as well as your own experiences. Then, put all of that information together to make an educated guess about what is *really* going on in the story.

Examples

- *If a character has sweaty palms, you could* **infer** *he is nervous.*
- *If a character never speaks up in class, you could* **infer** *she is shy.*
- *If a character gobbles up three burgers, you could* **infer** *he is hungry.*
- *If a character keeps coughing, you could* **infer** *she is getting sick.*
- *If a character has "a spring in his step," you could* **infer** *he is happy.*
- *If a character meets a magic fairy, you could* **infer** *she will get to make a wish.*

COMPREHENSION HELPER

Prediction

Using what you know from the text to make a smart guess about what will happen later on in a story.

TIP As you read a story, pause and play detective. Collect clues in the text and use them to make smart guesses about what will happen next. Making predictions keeps you actively engaged with the text and helps you better understand what you're reading.

Examples

- *I know that the castle is haunted, so I* **predict** *the main character will see a ghost.*
- *I know the wolf blew down the straw house, so I* **predict** *he will blow down the stick house, too.*
- *I know the main character is lonely, so I* **predict** *she will try to find a friend.*
- *I know the frog was a prince, so I* **predict** *he will turn into a prince again.*
- *I know the story takes place in a circus, so I* **predict** *there will be clowns.*

100 FIGURATIVE LANGUAGE TASK CARDS

FIGURATIVE LANGUAGE: IDIOMS

Saturday Chores

When my mom came into my room on Saturday morning, she **blew a gasket**. I looked around and didn't see anything wrong. Sure, a few pairs of pants were lying on my beanbag chair. And my bed was unmade. And there was a huge **mound** of shoes and shirts and books in the middle of the floor. And there was also a dirty cereal bowl on the dresser. But what was the big deal? She said my room was a **disaster area**. "Guess what you're doing today?" she said. "Uh, playing video games?" I said hopefully. I knew what I'd really be doing though: cleaning up my room!

KEY QUESTIONS

1. IDIOM ONE: What do you think *blew a gasket* means?

☐ sped up ☐ got mad ☐ cleaned up

2. IDIOM TWO: What do you think *disaster area* means?

☐ mess ☐ surprise ☐ game

3. CHALLENGE: Use *disaster area* in a sentence.

4. CONTEXT CLUES: What do you think *mound* means?

☐ a pair
☐ a neat stack
☐ a small mountain

5. S-T-R-E-T-C-H: Have you ever *blown a gasket* about something? What happened? Write about it.

FIGURATIVE LANGUAGE: IDIOMS

The Tortoise and the Hare

On your mark, get set, go! Hare started the race at a tremendously fast speed. Tortoise, who was usually as slow as molasses, got off to a **lumbering** start. "This is going to be **a piece of cake**," thought Hare. He grew so confident that he decided to relax beneath a tree. Then, **like a bolt out of the blue**, Tortoise rolled past. As Hare noted with horror, Tortoise was on a skateboard. Nothing in the race rules said you couldn't use a skateboard. Hare broke into a run. But it was too late. Tortoise rolled across the finish line to victory. Hare came in second.

KEY QUESTIONS

1. IDIOM ONE: What do you think *a piece of cake* means?

☐ sweet ☐ easy ☐ frosting

2. IDIOM TWO: What do you think *like a bolt out of the blue* means?

☐ sunny ☐ sudsy ☐ suddenly

3. CHALLENGE: Find another idiom in the story.

4. CONTEXT CLUES: What do you think *lumbering* means?

☐ wooden ☐ slow and awkward
☐ quick

5. S-T-R-E-T-C-H: Write a paragraph in which you use the idioms *a piece of cake* and *a bolt out of the blue*.

3

A Dose of Laughs

Karesha's granddad **adored** her. She was **the apple of his eye**. When he broke his leg and was stuck at home for several weeks, Karesha came by every day after school to visit him. Each day, she told him a new joke: *"What's the best time to buy a bird? When they're going cheap!"* and *"What do you call a cow that eats your grass? A lawn moo-er."* When he heard her jokes, Karesha's granddad giggled. "Why do you always tell me silly jokes?" he asked her. Karesha hugged him and said, "Because **laughter is the best medicine**, Grandpa!"

KEY QUESTIONS

1. IDIOM ONE: What do you think *the apple of his eye* means?

☐ much loved   ☐ crunchy   ☐ round

2. IDIOM TWO: What do you think *laughter is the best medicine* means?

☐ laughter makes you feel better
☐ laughter is free
☐ medicine is expensive

3. CHALLENGE: Use *laughter is the best medicine* in a sentence.

4. CONTEXT CLUES: What do you think *adored* means?

☐ visited   ☐ talked to   ☐ loved

5. S-T-R-E-T-C-H: Do you think *laughter is the best medicine*? Tell why or why not.

4

First-Day Jitters

On the first day of school, Jared found he was sitting beside a new kid named Alex. Alex didn't smile, or even look in his direction. Alex had a big dragon on his T-shirt, which seemed kind of scary. Jared started to feel kind of uncomfortable. But then, Alex made a silly face. And they both burst out laughing. That really helped **break the ice**. By the end of the first day, Jared and Alex were great friends.

At first, Jared had felt nervous around Alex. Alex had made him **anxious**. But Jared realized **you can't judge a book by its cover**.

KEY QUESTIONS

1. IDIOM ONE: What do you think *break the ice* means?

☐ make people nervous   ☐ go skating
☐ put people at ease

2. IDIOM TWO: What do you think *you can't judge a book by its cover* means?

☐ don't tell lies   ☐ read a lot
☐ something may be different than it first appears

3. CHALLENGE: Use *you can't judge a book by its cover* in a sentence.

4. CONTEXT CLUES: What do you think *anxious* means?

☐ comfortable   ☐ worried   ☐ forgetful

5. S-T-R-E-T-C-H: Make a list of things you can say to put people at ease.

FIGURATIVE LANGUAGE: IDIOMS

Besties!

Sasha and her best friend, Tia, are opposites. Sasha is **a night owl**. She likes to read late into the night, and she hates getting up in the morning. Tia, on the other hand, is **an early bird**. The morning is her favorite time of day. Sasha can be a little bit sloppy. Sometimes her shoes are untied and she doesn't even notice. Tia is very neat and tidy. Her hair is always pulled into a perfect bun. Sasha thinks cats make the best pets. Tia thinks dogs rule! But even though they are opposites in **numerous** ways, they each think the other is totally the best!

KEY QUESTIONS

1. IDIOM ONE: What do you think *a night owl* means?

- ☐ someone who stays up late
- ☐ someone who's smart
- ☐ someone who sleeps late

2. IDIOM TWO: What do you think *an early bird* means?

- ☐ someone who sings
- ☐ someone who is never late
- ☐ someone who gets up early

3. CHALLENGE: Use *night owl* in a sentence.

4. CONTEXT CLUES: What do you think *numerous* means?

☐ funny   ☐ many   ☐ strange

5. S-T-R-E-T-C-H: Besides *early bird*, there's another idiom in the fourth sentence. Can you find it? Use this idiom in a sentence of your own.

FIGURATIVE LANGUAGE: IDIOMS

When Pigs Fly

Josh really wanted to play the video game, but his big brother, Andre, wouldn't give him a turn. "When can I play?" asked Josh. "**When pigs fly**," answered Andre. Then Andre just kept right on playing. He looked to be having barrels of fun. It felt like Andre was **taunting** him. Josh was about to **call it a day**, when their dad walked into the room. "Andre, you need to finish mowing the lawn this instant," Dad said. Andre left, and Josh finally got his turn. Josh wouldn't have to wait until pigs could fly after all.

KEY QUESTIONS

1. IDIOM ONE: What do you think *when pigs fly* means?

☐ never   ☐ always   ☐ in a while

2. IDIOM TWO: What do you think *call it a day* means?

- ☐ remember
- ☐ use a phone
- ☐ give up

3. CHALLENGE: What other idiom can you find in the story?

4. CONTEXT CLUES: What do you think *taunting* means?

☐ jumping   ☐ finding   ☐ teasing

5. S-T-R-E-T-C-H: Make up an idiom that means *never*. Use it in a sentence.

FIGURATIVE LANGUAGE: IDIOMS

A Blessing in Disguise

Brothers Pedro and Tomás were supposed to go fishing. Pedro got up at 6 AM. When he checked, his brother was still fast asleep. Pedro shook Tomás awake. "Let me sleep," grumbled Tomás. So Pedro went back to his room feeling angry and bored. He was really **bent out of shape**. After a while, he picked up a book. He quickly became **engrossed**. Then, he heard thunder and it began pouring rain. Tomás refusing to get out of bed turned out to be a **blessing in disguise**. Today, Pedro would enjoy his book. The brothers could go fishing tomorrow.

KEY QUESTIONS

1. IDIOM ONE: What do you think *bent out of shape* means?

☐ lacking in exercise ☐ upset
☐ kneeling down

2. IDIOM TWO: What do you think *blessing in disguise* means?

☐ very sunny ☐ great costume
☐ good thing that seems bad at first

3. CHALLENGE: Use *blessing in disguise* in a sentence.

4. CONTEXT CLUES: What do you think *engrossed* means?

☐ deeply interested ☐ very sad
☐ quite disgusted

5. S-T-R-E-T-C-H: Make up three new idioms that mean *bent out of shape*.

FIGURATIVE LANGUAGE: IDIOMS

Sick Day

LuAnn woke up feeling **under the weather**. She had a slight headache and a runny nose. So she stayed home from school. Her mother tucked her under her cozy covers and brought her a warm cup of tea. Soon LuAnn felt well again. She watched her favorite movie. She read a great book. After school, her older brother came home. "How was your day?" he asked. "Great," LuAnn **blurted**, then she caught herself. "It was not so good," she said. "I had to stay home sick." Her brother grinned. "Sounds like you had a rough day," he laughed, "I sure hope you **get back on your feet** soon."

KEY QUESTIONS

1. IDIOM ONE: What do you think *under the weather* means?

☐ rained on ☐ happy ☐ ill

2. IDIOM TWO: What do you think *get back on your feet* means?

☐ wear nice sandals ☐ feel better
☐ stand up straight

3. CHALLENGE: Which of the previous two idioms best completes the sentence? I stayed in bed feeling _____.

4. CONTEXT CLUES: What do you think *blurted* means?

☐ walked backwards ☐ whispered
☐ said suddenly

5. S-T-R-E-T-C-H: Describe a time you were *under the weather*.

9

Up and Up

For his birthday, Max got an exciting gift: a ride in a hot air balloon. He invited his friend Luis to join him. At first, Luis was excited. But as the day of the balloon ride neared, he became **trepidatious**. He was nervous about being up so high. Luis kept his fear hidden from Max, and when Max picked him up, Luis pretended to be **as cool as a cucumber**. As he climbed into the balloon's basket, he had **butterflies in his stomach**. Then, as they went up and up, something unexpected happened. Luis forgot to be afraid. "Wow, this is awesome!" he exclaimed.

KEY QUESTIONS

1. IDIOM ONE: What do you think *as cool as a cucumber* means?

☐ calm ☐ excited ☐ nervous

2. IDIOM TWO: What do you think *butterflies in his stomach* means?

☐ a nervous feeling
☐ a happy feeling
☐ a sleepy feeling

3. CHALLENGE: Use *as cool as a cucumber* in a sentence.

4. CONTEXT CLUES: What do you think *trepidatious* means?

☐ happy ☐ fearful ☐ hungry

5. S-T-R-E-T-C-H: Have you ever had *butterflies in your stomach*? What caused them? Write about it.

10

Superpowers

Kami was **hanging out** with her three best pals. They were talking about which superpower they'd most like to have. Tina said she wanted to fly. She would soar up into the sky with the birds and she wouldn't have to take the bus to school. Carlos said he'd like to move things with his mind. Then he could clean up his room **in a snap**, just by thinking about it! Emily said she'd like to talk to animals. Then she could find out what her cat really thinks. Kami chose time travel. "Then I could **relive** all my favorite days—including this one!"

KEY QUESTIONS

1. IDIOM ONE: What do you think *hanging out* means?

☐ running around
☐ spending time together
☐ upside down

2. IDIOM TWO: What do you think *in a snap* means?

☐ quickly ☐ forever ☐ often

3. CHALLENGE: Use *in a snap* in a sentence.

4. CONTEXT CLUES: What do you think *relive* means?

☐ forget ☐ do again ☐ paint

5. S-T-R-E-T-C-H: What superpower would *you* like to have? Write about it.

FIGURATIVE LANGUAGE: IDIOMS

It's Not Rocket Science

Stu liked to **take it easy**. When he got a job at a hot dog stand, the owner asked him, "Can you cook hotdogs?" Stu answered: "Sure, that's no problem. **It's not rocket science**." He kept messing up, and soon lost the job. So he got another job, at a bookstore. The owner asked him, "Can you sell books?" Stu gave his **standard** answer: "It's not rocket science." Not surprisingly, that job didn't work out either. So Stu tried to get a job in a spaceship factory. "Can you make a Mars Rover?" asked the owner. "It's not rocket science," said Stu. "Actually, it is," said the owner, with a laugh.

KEY QUESTIONS

1. IDIOM ONE: What do you think *take it easy* means?

☐ get stressed out ☐ relax
☐ steal things

2. IDIOM TWO: What do you think *it's not rocket science* means?

☐ it's complex ☐ it's done on Earth
☐ it's easy

3. CHALLENGE: Use *it's not rocket science* in a sentence.

4. CONTEXT CLUES: What do you think *standard* means?

☐ usual ☐ silly ☐ angry

5. S-T-R-E-T-C-H: What job would you like to have when you grow up? Write about it.

FIGURATIVE LANGUAGE: IDIOMS

Bad Hair Day

Lisa went to the hair salon to get a haircut. She asked the stylist to trim just a little off the ends. But the stylist **went overboard**. Her scissors snipped and snipped, and when she was finished, most of Lisa's hair was in a pile on the floor. Lisa **gaped** at her reflection in the mirror and screamed, "My hair!" The stylist said it looked terrific, but Lisa knew the haircut was terrible. Even her mom agreed it wasn't great. "But here's the **silver lining**," her mom said. "Your head won't be hot this summer."

KEY QUESTIONS

1. IDIOM ONE: What do you think *went overboard* means?

☐ went swimming ☐ did a great job
☐ did too much

2. IDIOM TWO: What do you think *silver lining* means?

☐ good thing ☐ money ☐ nice haircut

3. CHALLENGE: Use *silver lining* in a sentence.

4. CONTEXT CLUES: What do you think *gaped* means?

☐ stared open-mouthed ☐ admired
☐ wouldn't look

5. S-T-R-E-T-C-H: Why does Lisa's mom say, "But here's the silver lining. Your head won't be hot this summer."?

Let It Snow!

All fall, Gabe had been waiting for snow. Finally, he woke up one December morning and saw that the ground outside was white. Gabe was **on cloud nine**. He threw on his clothes and ran outside to grab his sled. But just as he did, something terrible happened. It started to rain. This **took the wind out of his sails**. "Oh, no!" he shouted. If it kept up, the snow would melt. He went inside, but his dad had some good news. "It's going to get colder later today and they're **forecasting** a foot of snow!"

KEY QUESTIONS

1. IDIOM ONE: What do you think *on cloud nine* means?

☐ very uncertain ☐ very happy
☐ very snowy

2. IDIOM TWO: What do you think *took the wind out of his sails* means?

☐ made him happy ☐ made him sleepy
☐ disappointed him

3. CHALLENGE: Use *took the wind out of his sails* in a sentence.

4. CONTEXT CLUES: What do you think *forecasting* means?

☐ predicting ☐ snowing ☐ sledding

5. S-T-R-E-T-C-H: Can you find an idiom in the story about getting dressed?

Summer of Wonder

Summer was here and Hilary was . . . bored! What was she going to do all summer? Then she had an idea: She would make a **wish list**. She thought of ten new things she wanted to do. She would do one new thing each week. The first week, she decided to **branch out** and eat a different kind of food. So she and her dad went out for sushi. (So yummy!) The second week, she jogged two miles. (So tiring!) The third week, she got up really early to **behold** the sunrise. (So beautiful!) At the end of the summer she'd had ten new adventures, without even leaving town.

KEY QUESTIONS

1. IDIOM ONE: What do you think *wish list* means?

☐ plastic container
☐ list of things you want to do
☐ school supply list

2. IDIOM TWO: What do you think *branch out* means?

☐ try something new ☐ climb a tree
☐ eat sushi

3. CHALLENGE: Use *branch out* in a sentence.

4. CONTEXT CLUES: What do you think *behold* means?

☐ forget ☐ remember ☐ see

5. S-T-R-E-T-C-H: Write your wish list of ten things you'd like to do.

You Dream It, We Make It

The sign outside Larisa's store said: "You dream it, we make it." She was just putting the finishing touches on a very nice pair of leather shoes. As the customer walked in, Larisa held them up proudly. "Are you **pulling my leg**?" asked the customer. "How am I supposed to jump out of a plane using those?" Larisa was **baffled**. "I asked for a parachute," continued the customer. "You made me a pair of shoes." Larisa apologized, explaining that she'd misheard *parachute* as *pair of shoes*. The customer left, and Larisa started over—this time making a parachute. It was **back to the drawing board**.

KEY QUESTIONS

1. IDIOM ONE: What do you think *pulling my leg* means?

☐ dressing ☐ joking ☐ sleeping

2. IDIOM TWO: What do you think *back to the drawing board* means?

☐ time to start over
☐ time to stop
☐ time for lunch

3. CHALLENGE: Use *back to the drawing board* in a sentence.

4. CONTEXT CLUES: What do you think *baffled* means?

☐ angry ☐ silly ☐ confused

5. S-T-R-E-T-C-H: Has someone ever *pulled your leg*? Write about it.

Wally's Wallet

Wally had misplaced his wallet once again. If he didn't find it, he was going to be **in hot water**. He looked on his nightstand and under his bed. He checked beside the television, beneath the couch cushions, and above the kitchen sink. Wally even **inspected** the refrigerator, a place where he'd once left his wallet wrapped up with a half-eaten sandwich. Wally's wallet was nowhere to be found. This was beginning to feel like a **wild-goose chase**. "Have you checked your pocket?" asked his sister. Wally reached back and patted his pocket. There it was!

KEY QUESTIONS

1. IDIOM ONE: What do you think *in hot water* means?

☐ pleased ☐ hungry for soup
☐ in trouble

2. IDIOM TWO: What do you think a *wild-goose chase* means?

☐ hopeless search ☐ simple mistake
☐ funny walk

3. CHALLENGE: Use a *wild-goose chase* in a sentence.

4. CONTEXT CLUES: What do you think *inspected* means?

☐ destroyed ☐ carefully looked at
☐ lost

5. S-T-R-E-T-C-H: Think about your favorite books. Describe a scene in which a character finds him or herself *in hot water.*

Surprise, Surprise!

It was Friday. That very evening, a surprise party was planned for Nira. But as Kelly left school, she nearly **spilled the beans**. "See you tonight," said Kelly to her friend. "What?" asked Nira. "Oh, I meant see you Monday," said Kelly. "Hmmm," said Nira suspiciously. Fortunately, Kelly **clammed up** and didn't **reveal** anything more. That night, Nira's friends gathered and waited in a darkened room. Nira opened the door and turned on the light. Everyone yelled, "Surprise!" Nira nearly jumped through the roof. The plan had worked. Nira was REALLY surprised.

KEY QUESTIONS

1. IDIOM ONE: What do you think *spilled the beans* means?

☐ made a mess ☐ told the secret
☐ rode a trike

2. IDIOM TWO: What do you think *clammed up* means?

☐ paid money ☐ acted cool ☐ fell silent

3. CHALLENGE: Use *clammed up* in a sentence.

4. CONTEXT CLUES: What do you think *reveal* means?

☐ make known ☐ hide ☐ show off

5. S-T-R-E-T-C-H: Imagine that *spilled the ketchup* is an idiom. What would it mean?

Up in the Attic

When Stella's dad said she didn't have to clean her room today, it was **music to her ears**. Then he told her why: He wanted her to help him clean out the attic instead! Stella groaned. That chore sounded even worse than tidying her room. The attic was a mess. She and her dad **rummaged** through boxes. Stella found an old photo album of her dad's from when he was a kid. "Hey, look at this!" she said. As Stella and her dad looked through the photos, he told her about all the people from his past. "This is **a trip down memory lane**," he said with a grin.

KEY QUESTIONS

1. IDIOM ONE: What do you think *music to her ears* means?

☐ a favorite song ☐ a disappointment
☐ good news

2. IDIOM TWO: What do you think *a trip down memory lane* means?

☐ a distraction from cleaning
☐ a time to remember the past
☐ a way to fill old boxes

3. CHALLENGE: Use *a trip down memory lane* in a sentence.

4. CONTEXT CLUES: What do you think *rummaged* means?

☐ ran through ☐ laughed ☐ searched

5. S-T-R-E-T-C-H: Think of a time you heard something that was *music to your ears*. Write about it.

"You Can Say That Again"

Kyle had the strangest dream. In it, he met a table that was an actor. The table was getting ready to go on stage and perform. "**Break a leg**," said Kyle. "Thank you, kind sir," said the table. Next, he met a train having a temper tantrum. "**Pull yourself together**," said Kyle. "No, you can't make me," screamed the train. Then, Kyle walked past a cave. "You're having a **bizarre** dream, aren't you?" asked a voice from inside. "You can say that again," said Kyle. "You can say that again," echoed the voice, and it kept echoing until Kyle opened his eyes. Boy was he glad to be awake!

KEY QUESTIONS

1. IDIOM ONE: What do you think *break a leg* means?

☐ get well soon ☐ good luck
☐ wake up

2. IDIOM TWO: What do you think *pull yourself together* means?

☐ control your emotions
☐ get really excited
☐ blow your whistle

3. CHALLENGE: Find an idiom that means *I agree with you*.

4. CONTEXT CLUES: What do you think *bizarre* means?

☐ funny ☐ very strange ☐ happy

5. S-T-R-E-T-C-H: Write a mini-play starring the characters in this story.

Yo-Yo Expert

The package for Dottie's new yo-yo mentioned a website with an **instructional** video. But Dottie was eager to try out her yo-yo; she wanted to do the cool butterfly trick she'd seen. Immediately, the yo-yo got tangled. Somehow, it even got knotted up with her shoelaces. As she bent over to untie the knot, she fell over onto the floor. Talk about **adding insult to injury**. Who knew that such a simple toy could be so difficult? Dottie decided not to **cut corners** anymore. She sat down to watch the video and learned how to do the trick properly. Everyone loved the trick, which made Dottie as proud as a peacock.

KEY QUESTIONS

1. IDIOM ONE: What do you think *adding insult to injury* means?

☐ being super friendly
☐ making a bad situation worse
☐ making onlookers laugh

2. IDIOM TWO: What do you think *cut corners* means?

☐ do things quickly and badly
☐ do things carefully ☐ use scissors

3. CHALLENGE: Find another idiom in the story.

4. CONTEXT CLUES: What do you think *instructional* means?

☐ musical ☐ confusing ☐ teaching

5. S-T-R-E-T-C-H: Write about someone *adding insult to injury*.

Same Old Juan

When Malik's best friend, Juan, moved to a different city, Malik was **down in the dumps**. He and Juan had been pals ever since kindergarten. They were as close as brothers. Malik had other friends, but no one was quite like Juan. When summer came, Malik's mom said they were going to visit Juan and his family for a few days. At first, Malik was **apprehensive**. He wondered if Juan had changed in the months since they'd seen each other. But he quickly discovered that he was the **same old** Juan. Seeing his best friend was just like old times.

KEY QUESTIONS

1. IDIOM ONE: What do you think *down in the dumps* means?

☐ strange ☐ sad ☐ curious

2. IDIOM TWO: What do you think *same old* means?

☐ unfriendly
☐ same as before
☐ different than before

3. CHALLENGE: Use *down in the dumps* in a sentence.

4. CONTEXT CLUES: What do you think *apprehensive* means?

☐ nice ☐ worried ☐ funny

5. S-T-R-E-T-C-H: Have you ever been *apprehensive* about something? Write about it.

Super Sight

Nina had trouble seeing the board at school, so her mom took her to the eye doctor. The doctor asked Nina to read a bunch of letters on the wall. The bigger letters were **clear as day**. But as the letters got smaller, Nina struggled to read them. The doctor said Nina was nearsighted. She told Nina that a pair of glasses would **do the trick**. Nina wasn't crazy about getting glasses, though. No one else in her class wore them, and she worried that people would tease her. To her surprise, when she showed up **sporting** them a few days later, her friends said they wished they needed glasses, too!

KEY QUESTIONS

1. IDIOM ONE: What do you think *clear as day* means?

☐ very clear ☐ unclear ☐ daytime

2. IDIOM TWO: What do you think *do the trick* means?

☐ make people laugh ☐ fool people
☐ fix the problem

3. CHALLENGE: Use *do the trick* in a sentence.

4. CONTEXT CLUES: What do you think *sporting* means?

☐ listening ☐ wearing ☐ playing with

5. S-T-R-E-T-C-H: Find another sentence in the story with an idiom that tells how Nina feels about getting glasses.

Missing Mate

My mate and I sat in the laundry hamper, waiting to be washed. On laundry day, I got scooped up with all the other clothes and taken to the laundry room. My mate and I got separated, but it was **no big deal**. In the washer, I went round and round and the soap bubbles made me **spick-and-span**. Then I did somersaults in the dryer (my favorite part of wash day!). When it was time to get folded and put away, I waited to be **reunited** with my fellow red sock. But instead, I was on my own. My mate was missing. I sure hope they find my mate soon!

KEY QUESTIONS

1. IDIOM ONE: What do you think *no big deal* means?

☐ not a problem ☐ terrible ☐ clean

2. IDIOM TWO: What do you think *spick-and-span* means?

☐ folded up ☐ dry ☐ very clean

3. CHALLENGE: Write a sentence that uses the idiom *spick-and-span*.

4. CONTEXT CLUES: What do you think *reunited* means?

☐ brought back together ☐ washed
☐ tossed out

5. S-T-R-E-T-C-H: Can you think of five words that have the prefix *re-,* like *reunited*? List them.

Where's Duke?

When Imani's dog got loose and ran away, Imani was **brokenhearted**. Her family had gotten Duke when Imani was 6. Ever since, Duke had been her best pal. Whenever she came home from school, he always jumped up and down and **gleefully** wagged his tail. He followed her around, and he slept in her room at night. "Why would he run away?" Imani asked her mom. "Maybe he just wanted to explore the neighborhood," her mom said. "He'll be back." And in fact, just at that moment, Duke trotted into their yard. Imani screamed with joy when she saw his furry face. Duke was **a sight for sore eyes**!

KEY QUESTIONS

1. IDIOM ONE: What do you think *brokenhearted* means?

☐ poor ☐ excited ☐ very sad

2. IDIOM TWO: What do you think *a sight for sore eyes* means?

☐ something happy to see
☐ something sad to see
☐ something blurry to see

3. CHALLENGE: Use *a sight for sore eyes* in a sentence.

4. CONTEXT CLUES: What do you think *gleefully* means?

☐ sometimes ☐ happily ☐ always

5. S-T-R-E-T-C-H: How does Imani's mood change from the beginning to the end of the story? Why does it change?

25

Math Magic

Jack hated math. He liked all his other subjects: reading and writing, social studies, and science. But math was his **Achilles' heel**. There was something about working with numbers that he found **perplexing**. His friend Maya told him that he just needed to **put his nose to the grindstone** and do lots of practice. She offered to help him with some problems after school and to give him some tips when he got stuck. Pretty soon, Jack was getting the hang of it. And then something really weird happened. He discovered that he actually *liked* math!

KEY QUESTIONS

1. IDIOM ONE: What do you think *Achilles' heel* means?

☐ favorite topic ☐ weakness
☐ best subject

2. IDIOM TWO: What do you think *put his nose to the grindstone* means?

☐ move closer ☐ give up
☐ work hard

3. CHALLENGE: Use *put his nose to the grindstone* in a sentence.

4. CONTEXT CLUES: What do you think *perplexing* means?

☐ surprising ☐ hard to understand
☐ very funny

5. S-T-R-E-T-C-H: What's your *Achilles' heel*? Write about it.

26

Lights Out

After a long, **arduous** day of hiking with her mom, Lara was tired, so she **hit the hay** early. She was fast asleep when her two brothers began playing drums and guitar in their room, right next to hers. She ran in and said, "Hey! I'm trying to sleep!" They looked at her. "But it's only seven o'clock!" Lara crossed her arms and yelled, "Well, I'm tired!' Just then their dad came in and said he had the perfect solution. He handed Lara some earplugs. "Put these in your ears," he said. She did, and she crawled back into bed. Before long, she was **sleeping like a log**.

KEY QUESTIONS

1. IDIOM ONE: What do you think *hit the hay* means?

☐ went hiking ☐ went outside
☐ went to bed

2. IDIOM TWO: What do you think *sleeping like a log* means?

☐ sound asleep ☐ screaming
☐ wide awake

3. CHALLENGE: Use *sleeping like a log* in a sentence.

4. CONTEXT CLUES: What do you think *arduous* means?

☐ easy ☐ difficult ☐ quick

5. S-T-R-E-T-C-H: Imagine Lara didn't have earplugs. Can you think of another solution to her problem? Write about it.

Smart Umbrella

The year is 2100. A girl named Gamma is walking down the street in a big city. She walks past robots and cars that drive themselves. Suddenly, a storm breaks out. Soon, it's **raining cats and dogs**. "Blump it!" says Gamma. That's future slang for "Darn it!" Gamma **retrieves** her cellphone from her rocket backpack. She presses a button on her phone. A little invisible shield forms above her head. It blocks the raindrops—*plink, plink, plink*. Gamma is using her smart umbrella app. She thinks it's the **greatest thing since sliced bread**.

KEY QUESTIONS

1. IDIOM ONE: What do you think *raining cats and dogs* means?

☐ raining hard ☐ raining live animals
☐ raining in color

2. IDIOM TWO: What do you think *greatest thing since sliced bread* means?

☐ toaster oven ☐ best ever ☐ worst

3. CHALLENGE: Fill in the blanks.
_____ is the *greatest thing since sliced bread* because _____.

4. CONTEXT CLUES: What do you think *retrieves* means?

☐ gets ☐ breaks ☐ shouts

5. S-T-R-E-T-C-H: Make up an animal idiom for weather other than rain. Use it in a sentence.

Capture the Flag

Gary and Todd were playing a game called capture the flag. "I have a plan," said Gary. "**I'm all ears**," said Todd. Gary told Todd to go stand on his head. He should remain silent, no matter what. That would create a **diversion**. So Todd went and stood on his head. Soon, some kids from the other team crept up close. They asked Todd what he was doing, but he said nothing. They grew increasingly puzzled. Finally a kid reached out and tagged Todd. By then, it was too late. Gary had captured their flag. "That was **as easy as ABC**," said Gary, with a smile.

KEY QUESTIONS

1. IDIOM ONE: What do you think *I'm all ears* means?

☐ I'm listening closely
☐ I'm funny looking
☐ I'm ignoring what's said

2. IDIOM TWO: What do you think *as easy as ABC* means?

☐ difficult ☐ kind of easy ☐ super easy

3. CHALLENGE: Use *I'm all ears* in a sentence.

4. CONTEXT CLUES: What do you think *diversion* means?

☐ thing that makes others angry
☐ thing that redirects attention
☐ thing that's funny

5. S-T-R-E-T-C-H: Describe something that is *as easy as ABC*.

Diving Bee

The high dive looked like fun to Niko. But as soon as she climbed up there, she got nervous and started **having second thoughts**. The water was a long way down. Someone said, "Jump on the count of three!" When Niko got to three she stood, **petrified**. Someone said to try closing her eyes. That made it even worse. Then, a bee started buzzing around her. Yikes! Next thing Niko knew, she had jumped off the board. *Splash!* Niko swam to the side, got out, and got back in line for the high dive. Having that bee appear was **a stroke of luck**. Niko couldn't wait to do the high dive again!

KEY QUESTIONS

1. IDIOM ONE: What do you think *having second thoughts* means?

☐ eating ☐ doubting ☐ forgetting

2. IDIOM TWO: What do you think *a stroke of luck* means?

☐ a good occurrence ☐ a bad occurrence
☐ a strange occurrence

3. CHALLENGE: Which of the two previous idioms best completes the sentence? It was _____ that the rain started after our hike.

4. CONTEXT CLUES: What do you think *petrified* means?

☐ very brave ☐ filled with gasoline
☐ so frightened one can't move

5. S-T-R-E-T-C-H: Describe a situation in which you had *second thoughts*.

Scratchy Sweater

Jen's twin sister, Jada, always borrowed her clothes. Usually, the sisters were **like two peas in a pod**. But Jada's habit of never returning anything was frustrating. When Jada asked again to borrow a sweater, it was **the last straw**. Then Jen had a **devious** idea. She decided to lend Jada a very scratchy sweater. At school, Jen could see that Jada was itchy and uncomfortable. That evening, Jen said, "I hope you learned your lesson. You can borrow my clothes, but please give them right back." Jada agreed. The next morning, Jada borrowed Jen's favorite blouse. She returned it promptly that evening. The sisters never had any more clothes-borrowing problems.

KEY QUESTIONS

1. IDIOM ONE: What do you think *like two peas in a pod* means?

☐ very close ☐ different ☐ silly

2. IDIOM TWO: What do you think *the last straw* means?

☐ the final good thing
☐ the final delicious thing
☐ the final bad thing

3. CHALLENGE: Use *the last straw* in a sentence.

4. CONTEXT CLUES: What do you think *devious* means?

☐ sly ☐ dumb ☐ funny

5. S-T-R-E-T-C-H: Describe two friends who are *like two peas in a pod*.

Haircut Day

It was haircut day for Ned. Ned really hated getting haircuts. He wished he was the sort of dog whose hair didn't grow. But instead he was the kind of dog whose curly hair got long and shaggy. It grew until he looked as big as a bush. Every few months he had to go and get a haircut. The groomers would wash him and cut his hair and then blow him dry. And when it was all over, with most of his hair **shorn**, Ned looked as skinny as a string bean.

KEY QUESTIONS

1. SIMILE ONE: Find a simile about messy hair.

2. SIMILE TWO: Find a simile about being thin.

3. CHALLENGE: Make up a simile to describe being tall.

4. CONTEXT CLUES: What do you think *shorn* means?

☐ cut off
☐ washed and dried
☐ curled

5. S-T-R-E-T-C-H: Write a paragraph about a pet. Make sure it has at least three similes in it.

The Big, Bad, Poorly Informed Wolf

The Big Bad Wolf had done some internet research about the houses that pigs built. He learned that the houses were easy to blow down. He drove to a suburb where many pigs lived. He found what looked like a good house to destroy and stood before it. The Big Bad Wolf huffed like a raging hurricane. He puffed like a billowing smokestack. The house didn't budge. It was as strong as steel. The Big Bad Wolf soon grew **exhausted**. One of the pigs threw open the window and said, "Go home, Wolf." The pig added: "And don't believe everything you read on the internet."

KEY QUESTIONS

1. SIMILE ONE: Find a simile related to a storm.

2. SIMILE TWO: Find a simile related to something that's well-built.

3. CHALLENGE: Find one more simile in the passage.

4. CONTEXT CLUES: What do you think *exhausted* means?

☐ full of energy
☐ full of air
☐ very tired

5. S-T-R-E-T-C-H: Think of more similes to describe a huffing, puffing Big Bad Wolf. Make a list.

Sweet and Tart

At Maria's new house, there was a lovely apple tree in the backyard. The tree was as pretty as a picture. When summer arrived, small, green apples began appearing on the tree. Maria's dad said she had to wait until September to pick them, when they would be sweet. He said that now they would still be **tart**. But Maria was as impatient as a puppy. She was so excited to eat an apple from her very own tree that one day she couldn't wait any longer. She reached up, picked an apple, and bit into it. *Eww!* It was as sour as a lemon. Her dad was right.

KEY QUESTIONS

1. SIMILE ONE: Find a simile that means excited.

2. SIMILE TWO: Find a simile about a strong taste.

3. CHALLENGE: Find another simile in the story.

4. CONTEXT CLUES: What do you think *tart* means?

☐ sweet
☐ smooth
☐ sour

5. S-T-R-E-T-C-H: Have you ever had a hard time waiting for something? Write about it.

A Ferocious Beast

Marcos had a lively imagination. He hurried home as it was growing dark outside. Suddenly, he saw a creature coming toward him. In the dim light, it was hard to tell what this creature was. Its eyes were like a pair of flickering flames. It opened its mouth, revealing teeth as sharp as needles. The mystery creature crept closer and closer. Marcos was afraid it was going to **pounce on** him like a ferocious beast. "Meow," it said. "You're so little and cute," said Marcos, "but you sure gave me a scare." Then he knelt down and petted the kitten.

KEY QUESTIONS

1. SIMILE ONE: Find a simile related to fire.

2. SIMILE TWO: Find a simile related to sewing.

3. CHALLENGE: Find a simile about a wild animal.

4. CONTEXT CLUE: What do you think *pounce on* means?

☐ bounce
☐ suddenly attack
☐ snuggle

5. S-T-R-E-T-C-H: Describe a pet and use at least three similes.

The Itsy-Bitsy Spider

To people, the rain felt like a light drizzle. For itsy-bitsy Sal Spider, it was a major storm. He watched the Weather Channel on his tiny television. "Hurricane Hairy is moving through our area," shouted a spider newscaster. "Stay tuned to WebTV." The wind howled. Sal clung to his web. His eight legs were like tough metal clamps. Sal was soon **drenched**. Then, just like that, the storm ended. Out came the sun. Droplets of water formed on his web. They were as shiny as

 jewels. Sal did a happy, eight-legged jig. He had survived Hurricane Hairy!

KEY QUESTIONS

1. SIMILE ONE: Find a simile about Sal's legs.

2. SIMILE TWO: Find a simile about droplets of water.

3. CHALLENGE: Fill in the blanks to write similes. When the sun came out it was *as yellow as a/an* _____ and *as bright as a/an* _____.

4. CONTEXT CLUES: What do you think *drenched* means?

☐ scared
☐ dry
☐ very wet

5. S-T-R-E-T-C-H: Write a mini-story about a silly spider in which you use at least three similes.

A Green Breakfast

Makayla woke up in the morning as hungry as a lion. It was Saturday, which meant that her dad would make pancakes, her favorite! She went into the kitchen, and sure enough, there was her dad, standing at the stove. "Do you want some milk?" he asked. "Yes, please," Makayla said. Her dad poured her a glass of liquid that was as green as grass. Makayla stared at it, speechless. "Three pancakes, coming up!" he said. A minute later, he gave her a plate with three giant green pancakes on it. What was going on? "Happy St. Patrick's Day!" her dad said, **beaming**.

KEY QUESTIONS

1. SIMILE ONE: Find a simile that means you have a big appetite.

2. SIMILE TWO: Find a simile that mentions something you see outdoors.

3. CHALLENGE: Come up with a new simile to complete the sentence: Matt was *as hungry as* _____.

4. CONTEXT CLUES: What do you think *beaming* means?

☐ dancing   ☐ shouting   ☐ smiling

5. S-T-R-E-T-C-H: Make up a simile for every color of the rainbow: red, orange, yellow, green, blue, indigo (purple-blue), and purple.

The Kite

When Miguel woke up, the wind was blowing. "This weather is **ideal**," he said happily. Miguel loved windy days because then he could fly his kite at the open field near his house. Miguel loved his kite, which was as yellow as the sun. By the time he arrived at the field, the wind had died down. That made the kite fall to the ground. But soon the wind grew strong again. It lifted the kite so that it floated higher and higher and higher. The kite moved this way and that, like a dancer in the sky. Wow! Miguel loved flying his kite!

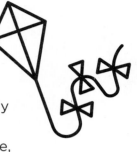

KEY QUESTIONS

1. SIMILE ONE: Find a simile related to a color.

2. SIMILE TWO: Find a simile about how something moves.

3. CHALLENGE: Write your own simile that describes a kite in the wind.

4. CONTEXT CLUES: What do you think *ideal* means?

☐ terrible
☐ windy
☐ perfect

5. S-T-R-E-T-C-H: Write a paragraph about something you love doing. Include at least two similes.

Nuts for Winter

Sam feels a chill in the air, and he starts to prepare for winter. Soon all the acorns will be gone, and the trees will be as bare as an empty cupboard. He gathers as many acorns as he can and buries them in spots around the forest. When winter comes, the air turns as icy as a freezer. But when Sam goes to look for his acorns, he can't remember where he buried them. He sees his friend Sadie, who has **an abundance** of nuts, more than she can eat. She tells him she'd be happy to share, and so Sam has plenty to eat the whole winter long. Hooray for Sadie!

KEY QUESTIONS

1. SIMILE ONE: Find a simile about the landscape in winter.

2. SIMILE TWO: Find a simile that describes the weather.

3. CHALLENGE: Make up a simile to describe something cold.

4. CONTEXT CLUES: What do you think *an abundance* means?

☐ an empty tree
☐ a small supply
☐ a large amount

5. S-T-R-E-T-C-H: Write a story about Sam's summer. In it, use at least three similes.

FIGURATIVE LANGUAGE: SIMILES

All Fixed!

When Anika was 6, she got a doll from her grandma. The doll was old and **fragile**. It had been her grandma's when she was a little girl. Anika took good care of the doll. It was special, like a treasure. She handled it gently, like a tiny bird. One day, as she showed the doll to her friend, one of the doll's legs came off. Anika had broken it! At first, she was very upset. Then her mother said they could take it to a shop where it could be fixed, as good as new. And that's exactly what they did!

KEY QUESTIONS

1. SIMILE ONE: Find a simile about something being special.

2. SIMILE TWO: Find a simile about the way Anika treated the old doll.

3. CHALLENGE: Create a new simile to describe a doll or toy.

4. CONTEXT CLUES: What do you think *fragile* means?

☐ new
☐ breakable
☐ different

5. S-T-R-E-T-C-H: Write about something that's like a treasure to you.

FIGURATIVE LANGUAGE: SIMILES

Fresh Cookies!

Emilio's mom baked chocolate chip cookies. Emilio smelled the **aroma** from his bedroom and ran into the kitchen as fast as a cheetah. "Can I have one?" he asked his mom. "Yes, but just one. You can have another one after dinner." Munch, crunch! Emilio ate his cookie as quick as a wink. Now he had to wait until after dinner for another. But the whole house smelled like cookies, and he couldn't concentrate on his homework. He went back to the kitchen. "Can I have just ONE more?" he asked his mom. She smiled and handed him a cookie. "I've already had two, myself!"

KEY QUESTIONS

1. SIMILE ONE: Find a simile that mentions an animal.

2. SIMILE TWO: Find a simile related to an eye.

3. CHALLENGE: Create a new simile related to an animal.

4. CONTEXT CLUES: What do you think *aroma* means?

☐ nice smell
☐ cookies
☐ kitchen

5. S-T-R-E-T-C-H: What's a food with a great aroma? Write about it and include at least two similes.

Frog Prince (Not)

Bella spied a frog sitting at the edge of a pond. She loved books, and, from **perusing** fairy tales, she knew all about frogs: Kiss one and he'll turn into a handsome prince. "I'll bet you'll have eyes as green as emeralds," said Bella. "*Ribbit*," said the frog. "I'll bet you'll have hair like spun gold," said Bella. "*Ribbit*," said the frog. "Okay, here goes," said Bella. She leaned down and planted a big, wet smooch right on the frog's lips. Bella waited . . . and waited. "*Ribbit*." This was no prince. It was just a frog. *Grrrr.* "I'll bet I was wrong," said Bella.

KEY QUESTIONS

1. SIMILE ONE: Find a simile about eyes.

2. SIMILE TWO: Find a simile about hair.

3. CHALLENGE: Create two new similes to complete the sentence: His eyes were *as blue as* _____ and his hair was as red as _____.

4. CONTEXT CLUES: What do you think *perusing* means?

☐ reading carefully
☐ watching
☐ ignoring

5. S-T-R-E-T-C-H: Write a paragraph describing a frog. In it, use at least three similes.

The Flimflam Man

"Behold this rare toy," said the **flimflam** man. "It comes from a faraway land." He held up a small, round glass ball for all the kids gathered around to see. "Buy this toy and you'll be as happy as a bunny with a carrot," said the flimflam man. "Buy it," he added, "and you'll be thrilled like the crowd at a circus." Then the flimflam man asked: "Who wants this amazing toy for just five dollars?" Excited kids rushed at him, waving their bills. One lucky boy got the toy. After everyone calmed down, he took a close look. It was only a marble.

KEY QUESTIONS

1. SIMILE ONE: Find a simile related to an animal.

2. SIMILE TWO: Find a simile related to entertainment.

3. CHALLENGE: Create two new similes to complete the sentence: S/he was *as happy as a/an* _____ and *as thrilled as a/an* _____.

4. CONTEXT CLUES: What do you think *flimflam* means?

☐ smart
☐ tricky
☐ tall

5. S-T-R-E-T-C-H: *Tall as a giraffe* is an example of another animal simile. Can you make up three more? Give it a try!

The Rescue

My little sister Avery and I were walking home from school when we saw an **injured** baby bird on the ground. It had fallen from its nest. I felt sorry for the bird, but I was in a hurry. I wanted to get home to watch my favorite show on TV. But Avery is as kind as an angel. She said we should go back to school and call someone who could help the bird. So we did. As fast as the wind, a wildlife specialist came out and rescued the little bird. I missed my TV show, but I'm glad I listened to Avery. She might be a little kid, but she's as wise as an owl.

KEY QUESTIONS

1. SIMILE ONE: Find a simile about being sweet and thoughtful.

2. SIMILE TWO: Find a simile about being intelligent.

3. CHALLENGE: Find another simile in the story.

4. CONTEXT CLUES: What do you think *injured* means?

☐ hurt
☐ small
☐ clumsy

5. S-T-R-E-T-C-H: Do you know someone who is wise? In what way? Write a paragraph about that person.

Shy Student

Tyler had to give a report in front of the whole class. He was terrified of talking in front of groups. He thought he would rather jump out of an airplane, or go swimming with sharks. Anything would be better than giving a presentation! His voice would **quiver** and his hands would sweat. "Everybody gets nervous," his friend Jamal told him. "Just practice a few times and it will be fine." When the day came, Tyler's knees shook like leaves in the wind. But he got through it, and everyone clapped. "You sounded like a pro," Jamal said. "Your voice was as smooth as silk."

KEY QUESTIONS

1. SIMILE ONE: Find a simile about a movement.

2. SIMILE TWO: Find a simile about how someone sounds.

3. CHALLENGE: Make up your own simile to describe someone who's nervous.

4. CONTEXT CLUES: What do you think *quiver* means?

☐ sing
☐ shake
☐ get low

5. S-T-R-E-T-C-H: Have you ever been nervous to speak in front of a group? If so, write about it. If not, tell about another time you were nervous.

A Surprise at the Zoo

Kayla and her family took a trip to the zoo. They looked at the lions, the gorillas, and the zebras. Then, suddenly, they saw a huge crowd of people. They all stood as still as statues. What were they looking at? Kayla wanted to find out! She pressed through the crowd until she got a **glimpse**. It was a brand-new baby elephant! She heard someone say that it was just two weeks old. The little elephant followed its mother around like a shadow. Kayla was excited that she got a chance to see the little elephant. Before long, it would be as big as a house!

KEY QUESTIONS

1. SIMILE ONE: Find a simile about not moving.

2. SIMILE TWO: Find a simile about following closely.

3. CHALLENGE: Find one more simile in the story.

4. CONTEXT CLUES: What do you think *glimpse* means?

☐ picture
☐ cramp
☐ look

5. S-T-R-E-T-C-H: Write a mini-story and include the simile *like a shadow* plus two original similes.

A Skating Lesson

Manny laced up his ice skates. Then he stepped out onto the rink. The ice was like a sea of polished glass. For a few minutes, he clung to the wall like a sticker. Then he was ready. Manny pushed off. For the briefest instant, he glided along. Then, as quick as a lightning strike, Manny was **sprawled** on the ice. He'd fallen. He wasn't hurt, just a little shaken. A woman skated up to Manny. "Are you here for lessons?" she asked. Manny looked up at her and grinned. "You bet I'm here for lessons," he said.

KEY QUESTIONS

1. SIMILE ONE: Find a simile about something being smooth.

2. SIMILE TWO: Find a simile about something happening fast.

3. CHALLENGE: Find another simile in this story.

4. CONTEXT CLUES: What do you think *sprawled* means?

☐ moving gracefully
☐ lying awkwardly
☐ jumping excitedly

5. S-T-R-E-T-C-H: Describe a winter scene using at least three similes.

Human Bowling

The acrobats saved their best trick for last. Ten of them in white tights formed into several rows. They were like a set of bowling pins. Another acrobat, dressed in black, somersaulted toward them. Faster and faster she tumbled. She was like a rolling bowling ball. She rolled through the rows of acrobats. As she **hurtled** past, they flipped and flopped as if they were bowling pins getting struck. When the trick ended, everyone was on the ground. They were like fallen pins. Then the acrobat in black stood up and declared: "Strike!" The audience was thrilled. The applause was as loud as thunder.

KEY QUESTIONS

1. SIMILE ONE: Find a simile about the acrobats in white tights.

2. SIMILE TWO: Find a simile about the acrobat dressed in black.

3. CHALLENGE: Find another simile in the passage.

4. CONTEXT CLUES: What do you think *hurtled* means?

☐ moved slowly
☐ moved at great speed
☐ stayed perfectly still

5. S-T-R-E-T-C-H: What other tricks might these silly acrobats do? Turn on your imagination and write about it, using at least two similes.

A Day at the Beach

Lily had been looking forward to a visit to the beach. When she arrived, she was **elated**. The sun was out. The sand was like a field of tiny, sparkling diamonds. The beach was crowded with happy people. Some of them lay under brightly colored umbrellas. "You don't want to end up as red as a lobster," said her mother, handing her a bottle of sunscreen. Lily put some on. She lay on the beach for awhile. Then she went in the ocean. It was as warm as a bath. She swam and splashed in the waves. What a perfect day!

KEY QUESTIONS

1. SIMILE ONE: Find a simile related to a color.

2. SIMILE TWO: Find a simile related to the ocean.

3. CHALLENGE: Find another simile in this story.

4. CONTEXT CLUES: What do you think *elated* means?

☐ bored
☐ confused
☐ thrilled

5. S-T-R-E-T-C-H: Describe a beach scene using at least three brand-new similes.

Ant Feast

Ari and Amber Ant were hard at work. They tried to lift a crumb of a cheese curl that had fallen on the sidewalk. For the tiny ants, the crumb was quite heavy. But the two ants were very strong. They were like a pair of tiny bodybuilders. Together, they lifted the crumb. They carried it back to their nest. Then they **gnawed** on it. Soon, other ants joined in the meal. The nest was like a cozy cottage. This single crumb provided enough food for everyone. It was like a big, tasty Thanksgiving feast.

KEY QUESTIONS

1. SIMILE ONE: Find a simile about two strong ants.

2. SIMILE TWO: Find a simile about a special and delicious meal.

3. CHALLENGE: Find another simile in the story.

4. CONTEXT CLUES: What do you think *gnawed* means?
- ☐ chewed
- ☐ hit
- ☐ carried

5. S-T-R-E-T-C-H: Write a bug mini-story in which you use at least three similes. Don't be afraid to get super silly!

Salty Treat

Essi was the new kid in school. She was from Finland, and she loved salty licorice. "Do you want to try a piece?" she asked Anna. "Sure," Anna said. She popped it in her mouth. The salt made her mouth as dry as a desert. The saltiness was mixed with bitterness. What an odd flavor, thought Anna. It hit her taste buds like fast-changing weather. It was pleasant, then unpleasant, then pleasant again. It was odd, all right, but also . . . strangely **scrumptious**. "I love salty licorice," announced Anna, adding: "Now, try a gumdrop, Essi! A gumdrop is like a little sugary explosion."

KEY QUESTIONS

1. SIMILE ONE: Find a simile about a dry mouth.

2. SIMILE TWO: Find a simile about a sweet flavor.

3. CHALLENGE: Find a third simile in the story.

4. CONTEXT CLUES: What do you think *scrumptious* means?
- ☐ horrible
- ☐ delicious
- ☐ sour

5. S-T-R-E-T-C-H: Describe your three favorite foods, using a simile for each. Example: *I love ice cream. It is as cold as the Arctic.*

S'mores Time

Elle was on a camping trip with her family. Night had fallen, and it was dark in the woods. She stared up at the sky. The full moon was a big hunk of tasty yellow cheese. The stars were little sparkly, sugar-dusted gumdrops. "Everything I see reminds me of food," thought Elle. Her stomach growled. Just then, her father **emerged** from the tent. He carried graham crackers, marshmallows, and chocolate. "Time to make s'mores," he said. His words were soothing music to Elle's very hungry tummy.

KEY QUESTIONS

1. METAPHOR ONE: Find a metaphor about something round in the sky.

2. METAPHOR TWO: Find a metaphor about things that twinkle in the sky.

3. CHALLENGE: Find a metaphor related to Elle's father.

4. CONTEXT CLUES: What do you think *emerged* means?

☐ jumped
☐ came out
☐ danced

5. S-T-R-E-T-C-H: Describe the night sky in your own words, using at least three metaphors.

City and Suburb

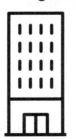

Monica lives in New York City. She lives on the 58th floor of a high-rise building. Her home has big windows, and she has awesome city views. But her bedroom is a shoebox. She doesn't mind because there's so much to do in the city. She even has a big park right outside her door. Her cousin Violet **resides** in the suburbs. Violet's house is a castle, with lots of big rooms, and her bedroom is huge! When Monica visits, they spend all their time doing fun stuff inside. But when Violet visits Monica, they go on outings and explore the city. The cousins love visiting each other and seeing another side of life.

KEY QUESTIONS

1. METAPHOR ONE: Find a metaphor about something small.

2. METAPHOR TWO: Find a metaphor about something large.

3. CHALLENGE: Make up your own metaphor about the city or the suburbs and use it in a sentence.

4. CONTEXT CLUES: What do you think *resides* means?

☐ remembers
☐ visits
☐ lives

5. S-T-R-E-T-C-H: Write a paragraph about your favorite place. In it, use at least two metaphors.

53

My Robot, Rob

My robot, Rob, has lots of different skills. For example, he's very good at sports. When we play basketball, Rob leaps high into the air, and he's a **bounding** kangaroo. "Beep, beep. Score!" he says. My robot is also great at eating. Give him any food, even broccoli, and he'll gobble it up in a flash. "Beep, beep. That was divine!" he says. Rob is a bottomless pit, I tell you. My robot is a talented dancer, too. When waltzing, he's a graceful gazelle. What else is Rob good at? Math, of course. Ask him what 45 x 23 x 87 equals and he'll instantly reply, "Beep, beep. The correct answer is 90,045!" My robot, Rob, is a shining star. Beep, beep.

KEY QUESTIONS

1. METAPHOR ONE: Find a metaphor related to being good at basketball.

2. METAPHOR TWO: Find a metaphor related to eating a lot.

3. CHALLENGE: Find two more metaphors in the story.

4. CONTEXT CLUES: What do you think *bounding* means?

☐ leaping upward
☐ climbing down
☐ lying around

5. S-T-R-E-T-C-H: Write a mini-biography of yourself. In it, use at least three metaphors.

54

Different Weather

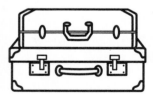

When Ping went to visit her aunt in Arizona, she was in for a surprise. She and her family left Oregon in the middle of a rainstorm. As they drove to the airport, the rain was a thick curtain of water. It was chilly, too. Ping packed her rain jacket and a couple of warm sweaters. When they came out of the airport in southern Arizona, they walked into a giant oven. It was **sweltering**! A sign said it was 101 degrees. Ping looked down at her jeans and rain boots. "I packed all wrong," she said. "Don't worry," her mom said. "I packed some shorts and T-shirts, and your swimsuit, too!"

KEY QUESTIONS

1. METAPHOR ONE: Find a metaphor about bad weather.

2. METAPHOR TWO: Find a metaphor about heat.

3. CHALLENGE: Make up a metaphor about heat.

4. CONTEXT CLUES: What do you think *sweltering* means?

☐ pouring
☐ very hot
☐ chilly

5. S-T-R-E-T-C-H: What is your favorite kind of weather? Tell why you like it.

Kurt's Game

My brother Kurt is really tall. He's the tallest kid in his entire high school. Wherever he goes, people always ask Kurt if he plays basketball. He doesn't. For Kurt, basketball is a shoe that doesn't fit. He doesn't like the game. Baseball is another story. With baseball, Kurt is a fish in water. Nothing makes him happier than standing on the pitcher's mound, throwing strikes across the plate. I'm sure he could be an **exceptional** basketball player, but Kurt says you have to do what you love.

KEY QUESTIONS

1. METAPHOR ONE: Find a metaphor that mentions something you wear.

2. METAPHOR TWO: Find a metaphor that mentions an animal.

3. CHALLENGE: Create a metaphor to describe your favorite sport.

4. CONTEXT CLUES: What do you think *exceptional* means?

☐ very tall
☐ unhappy
☐ excellent

5. S-T-R-E-T-C-H: What's something you do because you love it? Write about it and use a metaphor.

A Book of Poetry

Hank Hound and Pam Poodle were on a date. "Your eyes are two twinkling stars gracing the night sky," said Hank. "Your fur is puffy clouds floating in the heavens." Blushing, Pam said: "You have such a way with words, Hankie. You're a regular book of poetry." The waiter set down their doggie bowls. Suddenly, Hank kneeled, a golden collar **clutched** in one paw and asked, "Will you be my doggie bride?" But before Pam could answer, a car drove past the restaurant. Hank rushed outside and chased the car down the street, barking, *"Woof, woof, woof!"*

KEY QUESTIONS

1. METAPHOR ONE: Find a metaphor about a facial feature.

2. METAPHOR TWO: Find another metaphor about Pam Poodle.

3. CHALLENGE: Find a metaphor that describes Hank.

4. CONTEXT CLUES: What do you think *clutched* means?

☐ held loosely
☐ dropped
☐ held tightly

5. S-T-R-E-T-C-H: Turn on your imagination and write three metaphors by filling in the blanks: Your eyes are _____ and your nose is _____ and your mouth is _____.

Beach Bliss

One hot summer day, my family decided to escape the **scorching** temperatures and go to the beach. The ocean breeze was a giant fan that cooled us off in no time flat. For my little brother, Ty, the beach is a great big sandbox. He brought his pail and shovel and played for hours! My older sister loves the beach, too. She spent the whole time jumping over the waves as they rolled into the shore. As for me, the beach is my favorite library. I sat in a beach chair under our umbrella and read my favorite books all afternoon. It was the perfect summer day.

KEY QUESTIONS

1. METAPHOR ONE: Find a metaphor for the wind.

2. METAPHOR TWO: Find a metaphor that tells how Ty views the beach.

3. CHALLENGE: Find another metaphor about the beach.

4. CONTEXT CLUES: What do you think *scorching* means?

☐ nice and cool
☐ very hot
☐ rainy

5. S-T-R-E-T-C-H: Write a paragraph about the beach. In it, use at least two metaphors.

A Roller-Coaster Day

Jorge forgot to study for the test. Luckily, when he arrived at class, there was a substitute teacher. The test had been **postponed** until the next day. During gym, Jorge played basketball. He missed an important late-game shot. But a player on the other team also missed. Then Jorge made the winning shot. He was king of the world! After school, Jorge missed the bus and had to walk home. He felt sad and stared

at the ground. He saw a $10 bill lying there. When he got home, his mother asked: "How was your day?" Jorge answered: "It was a real roller coaster."

KEY QUESTIONS

1. METAPHOR ONE: Find a metaphor related to Jorge's winning shot.

2. METAPHOR TWO: Find a metaphor related to Jorge's entire day.

3. CHALLENGE: Imagine a game where one team won 24–0. Fill in the blank with a metaphor, "The game was a _____."

4. CONTEXT CLUES: What do you think *postponed* means?

☐ missed
☐ put off to a later date
☐ forgotten

5. S-T-R-E-T-C-H: Turn on your imagination and write a paragraph about a day that was "a real roller coaster."

Night Chicken

Chad's older brother, Ben, stayed up late. Ben was a real night bat. Chad wanted to be like Ben. So he decided to stay up all night. Sometime after 2 a.m., Chad glanced out his bedroom window. The full moon was an enormous eyeball. Chad tried to ignore the moon, but it gave him a jittery feeling. So he **scurried** down the hallway and woke up Ben. Ben calmed his little brother down. Soon, Chad drifted off to sleep. The next morning, he came to a conclusion. Ben was a night bat, and Chad was a night chicken.

KEY QUESTIONS

1. METAPHOR ONE: Find a metaphor related to a mammal.

2. METAPHOR TWO: Find a metaphor about an object in the night sky.

3. CHALLENGE: Find a metaphor related to a bird.

4. CONTEXT CLUES: What do you think *scurried* means?

☐ stomped
☐ jumped
☐ hurried

5. S-T-R-E-T-C-H: Turn on your imagination and make up your own animal metaphor. Then use it in a sentence, and explain what it means.

Visiting Granddad

Every weekend, Nora and her mom went to visit Nora's granddad. Visits with him were trips in a time machine. Her granddad grew up on a farm in Norway, and **regaled** Nora with stories about his life before he moved to America. Nora loved hearing about life in Norway. She especially loved hearing about the changing light. In summer, it remains light outside until midnight. But in winter, the days are a dark cave, and it's only light for a very short time. Nora hoped to visit Norway some day and see her grandfather's home for herself.

KEY QUESTIONS

1. METAPHOR ONE: Find a metaphor about Nora's visits with her granddad.

2. METAPHOR TWO: Find a metaphor about the days of winter.

3. CHALLENGE: Make up your own metaphor about darkness.

4. CONTEXT CLUES: What do you think *regaled* means?

☐ tickled
☐ bored
☐ entertained

5. S-T-R-E-T-C-H: Write about someone you like talking with. Tell what makes that person special and use at least one metaphor.

My Teenage Brother

It happened out of nowhere. One day, my brother Matt woke up and was suddenly hungry *all the time*. He was hungry when he woke up, so he'd eat a big breakfast, and an hour later he'd be hungry again. When we went out for pizza, Matt didn't have just two or three slices. He had ten! One day I made some cookies, and Matt was a giant vacuum, sucking them up in no time flat. My mom said he was just going through a growth spurt. And she was right. He was a fast-growing beanstalk. By the end of the summer, he had **surpassed** my dad in height!

KEY QUESTIONS

1. METAPHOR ONE: Find a metaphor about eating cookies.

2. METAPHOR TWO: Find a metaphor about Matt's growth spurt.

3. CHALLENGE: Make up your own metaphor about someone who's hungry.

4. CONTEXT CLUES: What do you think *surpassed* means?

- ☐ fooled
- ☐ went beyond
- ☐ changed

5. S-T-R-E-T-C-H: Write a paragraph about food. Include at least two metaphors.

Harry the Hurricane

Charlotte and her dad went to the rescue shelter to pick out a dog to bring home. There were lots of cute pups to choose from, but Charlotte fell in love with a little brown-and-white one named Harry. At first when they brought Harry home, he was **timid** and scared. "Right now, he's a turtle in his shell," Charlotte's dad said. "But he'll warm up in time." And boy, did he ever! After a few weeks, Harry felt right at home. When Charlotte took him outside, Harry ran and jumped and made big messes. He was a fast-moving hurricane. It was hard to believe he'd ever been timid!

KEY QUESTIONS

1. METAPHOR ONE: Find a metaphor about being shy.

2. METAPHOR TWO: Find a metaphor about being speedy.

3. CHALLENGE: Make up a metaphor about someone who's fearful.

4. CONTEXT CLUES: What do you think *timid* means?

- ☐ shy
- ☐ silly
- ☐ angry

5. S-T-R-E-T-C-H: What are some things people can do when they're feeling shy? Make a list!

Amazing Colors

Aki and his grandparents took a car trip to go see the Grand Canyon. Aki knew that the Grand Canyon would be an amazing sight. It was more than a mile from the top of the canyon down to the river at the bottom. What surprised Aki was how beautiful it was. Most of the canyon rock was deep red, but parts were green and gray and violet. Late in the day, when the sun set, the canyon walls were a colorful kaleidoscope. The sky above was pink cotton candy. Aki took lots of pictures so he would never forget this **gobsmacking** sight!

KEY QUESTIONS

1. METAPHOR ONE: Find a metaphor related to something you look through.

2. METAPHOR TWO: Find a metaphor related to a treat.

3. CHALLENGE: Make up a metaphor that describes the sky.

4. CONTEXT CLUES: What do you think *gobsmacking* means?

☐ scary
☐ very funny
☐ amazing

5. S-T-R-E-T-C-H: Write about something you've seen that was *gobsmacking*.

Lost in a Book

Ana's younger brother, Timmy, had just turned four. He was having a birthday party at their family's home. All his little friends were there. A clown blew up balloons. Kids ran and jumped and shouted and spilled drinks. Ana's home was a zoo! She helped blow out Timmy's candles. She joined in singing "Happy Birthday" to him. Then, she slipped off to her silent bedroom. She lay on her bed, picked up a book she'd been enjoying, and started a new chapter. What a relaxing and **tranquil** break from Timmy's party. Ana's book was a peaceful land that she could get lost in.

KEY QUESTIONS

1. METAPHOR ONE: Find a metaphor related to Ana's home.

2. METAPHOR TWO: Find a metaphor related to reading.

3. CHALLENGE: Imagine a room where everyone is noisily running around. Create your own metaphor by filling in the blank: The room was a/an _____.

4. CONTEXT CLUES: What do you think *tranquil* means?

☐ loud   ☐ calm   ☐ silly

5. S-T-R-E-T-C-H: Ana's book was a "tranquil land that she could get lost in." Dream up a metaphor for a book that's funny, scary, or sad.

Princess Poppy Leaves the Castle

No matter the season, Princess Poppy liked to stay inside the castle playing video games. When summer came, the queen said, "Go outside. The sun is a warm, happy friend smiling down on you." Princess Poppy shook her head. Autumn arrived. "Go outside," said the queen. "The leaves are little ballerinas twirling in the air." Princess Poppy shook her head. Winter arrived. "Go outside," said the queen. "The snowflakes are video game aliens coming down to Earth." Now that sounded **appealing**! Princess Poppy bundled up in her royal winter wear, and rushed outside to play in the snow.

KEY QUESTIONS

1. METAPHOR ONE: Find a metaphor about summer weather.

2. METAPHOR TWO: Find a metaphor about fall weather.

3. CHALLENGE: Find a metaphor about winter weather and then make up your own.

4. CONTEXT CLUES: What do you think *appealing* means?

☐ cold and lonely
☐ good and interesting
☐ bad and boring

5. S-T-R-E-T-C-H: Metaphors are good for describing seasons, such as spring: *The flowers are a crowd in brightly colored clothing.* Make up one metaphor for each of the four seasons.

Hot Sauce

Niles and Ozzy had a hot-sauce-eating contest. The first sauce they tried was called Pure Pepper Pain. Both boys agreed that it was almost **unbearably** hot. Next, they tried one called Red Rage. "Yowza, this is hot!" said Niles. "My mouth is an oven turned up to 400 degrees." Ozzy said: "Kaboom, my mouth is a volcano blowing its top." They were like panting dogs with their tongues hanging out. The sauce was so hot that beads of sweat formed on the boys' foreheads. "Should we keep going?" asked Niles. "Yes, let's," said Ozzy. "This is a lot of fun."

KEY QUESTIONS

1. METAPHOR ONE: Find a metaphor related to something found in a kitchen.

2. METAPHOR TWO: Find a metaphor related to a natural disaster.

3. CHALLENGE: A simile compares two things using *like or as*. For instance: "They were like panting dogs with their tongues hanging out." Turn this simile into a metaphor.

4. CONTEXT CLUES: What do you think *unbearably* means?

☐ not able to be tolerated
☐ not related to bears ☐ lots of fun

5. S-T-R-E-T-C-H: Dream up a hot sauce name. Then use a metaphor to describe how it makes your mouth feel.

Who's There?

Ava's family was on vacation. After a long day of hiking, they came back to their cabin and fell into their beds. Ava was **enervated**, and the  bed was a soft, fluffy cloud. She was almost asleep when she heard a scratching sound. She looked around the room, but it was pitch black. She heard the noise again. Outside, the wind was a howling wolf. "Is somebody there?" she nervously called out. The next minute she heard the sound once more. It was right outside her window! She parted the curtain and saw a tiny raccoon. *Phew!* And with that she fell asleep.

KEY QUESTIONS

1. METAPHOR ONE: Find a metaphor that describes something comfortable.

2. METAPHOR TWO: Find a metaphor about the weather.

3. CHALLENGE: Make up your own metaphor for the wind.

4. CONTEXT CLUES: What do you think *enervated* means?

☐ very hungry
☐ out of energy
☐ too busy

5. S-T-R-E-T-C-H: Imagine a different ending to this story. Now write it, and include your own metaphor.

A Graceful Swan

I'm pretty good at science, and my teacher says I have a talent for drawing, but when it comes to dancing, forget about it! On the other hand, my sister Lucy is an amazing dancer. She has been taking ballet lessons for 10 years, ever since she was four years old, and wow, is she good! When she dances, she's a graceful swan gliding across the stage. Last week, we went to see her in a big performance. Everyone was great, but Lucy was the **standout**. After she did her solo part, the audience was a symphony of clapping hands. I was so proud of my sister!

KEY QUESTIONS

1. METAPHOR ONE: Find a metaphor about Lucy's sister.

2. METAPHOR TWO: Find a metaphor about the people watching.

3. CHALLENGE: Make up another metaphor about someone dancing.

4. CONTEXT CLUES: What do you think *standout* means?

☐ silly one
☐ especially good one
☐ clumsy one

5. S-T-R-E-T-C-H: What are you good at? What are you not good at? Write about both.

Moira and Melvin at the Movies

Devon was at the movie theater. Even though it was dark, he was sure that his friends Moira and Melvin were there, too. How did he know? Well, it was a funny movie, and he recognized their laughs. Moira's laugh was a tinkling piano floating on a summer breeze. Melvin's laugh was a hyena that had eaten too much sugar. Up on the screen, another funny thing happened in the movie. Soon the theater was filled with a **raucous** "*HAR! HAR! HAR!*" Under that, it was just possible to hear a quiet "*tee, hee, hee.*" Yes, Moira and Melvin were at the movies.

KEY QUESTIONS

1. METAPHOR ONE: Find a metaphor involving a musical instrument.

2. METAPHOR TWO: Find a metaphor involving a wild animal.

3. CHALLENGE: Which laugh is Melvin's? How do you know?

4. CONTEXT CLUES: What do you think *raucous* means?

☐ loud and wild
☐ quiet and calm
☐ funny and silly

5. S-T-R-E-T-C-H: Fill in the blanks to write your own metaphor.
My friend Luisa has a funny laugh. It makes this sound: _____.
Her laugh is a/an _____.

Johnny Flower Seed

Lacey was helping her mother with the garden. Her messy toddler brother, Johnny, wanted to help, too. He grabbed a handful of pansy seeds. First, he sprinkled them in the soil of the garden. But Johnny was a nonstop spinning top. He **whirled** through the backyard, scattering seeds. Several weeks passed, and Lacey looked out the window. The pansies had popped up, and they weren't only in the garden. They were everywhere! The backyard was a colorful painting come to life. *Leave it to Johnny to make a big mess*, thought Lacey, *but at least this mess is beautiful!*

KEY QUESTIONS

1. METAPHOR ONE: Find a metaphor about Johnny.

2. METAPHOR TWO: Find a metaphor related to flowers.

3. CHALLENGE: Fill in the blank with another metaphor that uses *nonstop*.
S/he was a nonstop _____.

4. CONTEXT CLUES: What do you think *whirled* means?

☐ made a buzzing sound
☐ spun round and round
☐ tiptoed

5. S-T-R-E-T-C-H: Imagine someone was the opposite of Johnny, very low energy. Dream up a metaphor to describe that person.

Opportunity Knocks

Will had been saving for a new baseball glove. He needed only $5 more. One day, his toddler sister ate crackers while she watched a TV show. Crumbs were **strewn** all over the floor. Just then, his mother walked in. "This rug needs a good cleaning," she said. Opportunity was knocking! This was the chance Will had been waiting for. "I'll do it for $5," he offered. "You have a deal," said his mom. Will got the vacuum. The vacuum hummed as Will pushed it back and forth. Soon the floor was so clean that it beamed. Will smiled as he headed to the store to buy his new glove.

KEY QUESTIONS

1. PERSONIFICATION ONE: Find an example of personification related to a chance to do something.

2. PERSONIFICATION TWO: Find an example of personification related to a sound.

3. CHALLENGE: Find another example of personification in the story.

4. CONTEXT CLUES: What do you think *strewn* means?

☐ stuck ☐ swept ☐ scattered

5. S-T-R-E-T-C-H: Write a paragraph about a time that "opportunity knocked" for you. Use two examples of personification.

No Time for Boredom

Over the summer, Tilda went to visit her grandparents for two whole weeks. They lived in a house in the woods. There was a tall tree standing guard out in front, and in back there were flower gardens, and a tire swing hanging from a tree branch. There was no TV or internet, and Tilda worried that she would get bored. But there was no time for boredom! In the morning, she fed the chickens, then went swimming in the lake. At night, she took walks with her grandparents and **gazed** up at the stars winking overhead. When it was time to leave, Tilda was already planning her next visit.

KEY QUESTIONS

1. PERSONIFICATION ONE: Find an example of personification about something in the yard.

2. PERSONIFICATION TWO: Find an example of personification about something in the sky.

3. CHALLENGE: Write a sentence that includes a personification of a tree.

4. CONTEXT CLUES: What do you think *gazed* means?

☐ winked
☐ yelled
☐ looked

5. S-T-R-E-T-C-H: What are some things you like to do when you unplug from TV and the internet? Write about it.

Yard Sale

Jake's neighbors had a yard sale. They put up a huge sign that screamed "Bargains!" and they put out lots of stuff they wanted to get rid of. Jake and his dad stopped by to look at all the items. Jake's dad said the mystery novels were calling to him, and he browsed through several piles. Jake looked at an old chair that groaned when he sat down in it. There were lamps, books, broken dolls, and other **arbitrary** items. Then Jake spotted a baseball glove. He tried it on. It was just his size. And it was only two dollars. The glove lived on Jake's hand the rest of the summer!

KEY QUESTIONS

1. PERSONIFICATION ONE: Find an example of personification about books.

2. PERSONIFICATION TWO: Find an example of personification about a piece of furniture.

3. CHALLENGE: Find two more examples of personification in this story.

4. CONTEXT CLUES: What do you think *arbitrary* means?

☐ new
☐ home
☐ random

5. S-T-R-E-T-C-H: Make up personifications for these pieces of furniture: a desk, a bed, a table, a lamp.

A Boring Summer

It was Jaycee's first day of school. "Class, I'd like you each to write an essay about your summer," said her teacher. "You have 20 minutes." Jaycee thought that, sadly, it had been a boring summer. The days had slowly strolled by. What could Jaycee even write? Well, she'd gone to camp. She had swum at the pool. Soon, her pencil raced across her paper. Oh, she couldn't forget her new bike, which she had ridden everywhere. The bike had been her loyal friend. "Time's up," said the teacher. The 20 minutes had gone by like a flash. Jaycee hadn't even written half of what she'd done. Maybe it wasn't such a **humdrum** summer after all.

KEY QUESTIONS

1. PERSONIFICATION ONE: Find an example of personification related to the summer.

2. PERSONIFICATION TWO: Find an example of personification related to writing.

3. CHALLENGE: Find another example of personification in the story.

4. CONTEXT CLUES: What do you think *humdrum* means?

☐ exciting
☐ uneven
☐ boring

5. S-T-R-E-T-C-H: Write a mini-story about a lively pencil, using at least three instances of personification.

Mister Goofball to the Rescue

The lightning leaped across the sky. The thunder grumbled. That was when little Kamal crawled under the bed. He huddled there, very frightened. This is what he always did during thunderstorms. His big sister Riya knew that she needed to **distract** him. So she went and found Mister Goofball. That was a puppet that Kamal loved. She set Mister Goofball on the floor near the bed. After a few minutes, Kamal came out from under the bed. He picked up the puppet. The angry storm kept raging, but happy Kamal just kept playing.

KEY QUESTIONS

1. PERSONIFICATION ONE: Find an example of personification related to something you see during a storm.

2. PERSONIFICATION TWO: Find an example of personification related to something you hear during a storm.

3. CHALLENGE: Find a sentence in the story that contains two examples of personification.

4. CONTEXT CLUES: What do you think *distract* means?

☐ tickle
☐ explain
☐ amuse

5. S-T-R-E-T-C-H: Write a mini-story about the weather using lots of personification.

The Big Trip

Vivian and her family were going on vacation. This would be Vivian's first time ever on an airplane. The night before, she was so excited she could hardly sleep. But on the way to the airport, they hit heavy traffic. Her dad stepped on the brake, and the car sighed as it came to a stop. "Oh, no!" Vivian **shrieked**. "Are we going to miss our plane?" Soon the cars began their march down the highway again. They made it to the airport in plenty of time. Vivian would soon be 30,000 feet in the air. She couldn't wait!

KEY QUESTIONS

1. PERSONIFICATION ONE: Find an example of personification related to the car Vivian is in.

2. PERSONIFICATION TWO: Find an example of personification related to the other cars on the highway.

3. CHALLENGE: Use personification to describe Vivian's suitcase.

4. CONTEXT CLUES: What do you think *shrieked* means?

☐ laughed
☐ screamed
☐ pretended

5. S-T-R-E-T-C-H: Where would you like to travel to on a plane? Write about it.

Snorg's Halloween

Snorg was a shy young monster. At sunset, he peered out his window. The sun slipped below the horizon to sleep for the night. The moon gazed down. Soon, ghosts, zombies, and witches filled the sidewalk in front of his house! Suddenly, the doorbell screamed, *"Ding-dong!"* Snorg felt terrified. "It's Halloween," explained his monster mommy. "Tonight, the humans dress up like spooky creatures." Snorg whimpered: "What do I do?" His mother answered: "Just give them treats." Snorg opened the door. All evening, he handed out sweet treats. He even **doled out** goodies to some humans dressed up as monsters!

KEY QUESTIONS

1. PERSONIFICATION ONE: Find an example of personification related to the sun.

2. PERSONIFICATION TWO: Find an example of personification related to the moon.

3. CHALLENGE: Find another example of personification in the story.

4. CONTEXT CLUES: What do you think *doled out* means?

☐ ate up
☐ handed out
☐ took

5. S-T-R-E-T-C-H: What is your favorite costume to wear? Write about it.

Banana Bungle

Zoey Powers was an actor. She took herself very seriously. Today, Zoey tried out for a movie. To show off

her skills, she made a serious face and a funny face. Then, she puckered up her lips to look **romantic**. "This is great stuff," said the movie director. "The camera loves you." By now, Zoey felt very confident. She decided to show off her dance moves. As she shimmied, she stepped on a banana peel and flipped up in the air. Lying on the ground, Zoey thought: "The camera may love me, but that banana peel hates me."

KEY QUESTIONS

1. PERSONIFICATION ONE: Find an example of personification related to a camera.

2. PERSONIFICATION TWO: Find an example of personification related to a fruit.

3. CHALLENGE: Fill in the blanks to invent two new examples of personification. The camera _____ and the banana peel _____.

4. CONTEXT CLUES: What do you think *romantic* means?

☐ happy   ☐ sad   ☐ in love

5. S-T-R-E-T-C-H: What happens next in the story? Write it and use personification.

Watching the Weather

For weeks, James eagerly **anticipated** his birthday party at the amusement park. He and his friends would go on all the rides and eat pizza and ice cream. It was the best day he could imagine. But on the morning of his party, the weather didn't cooperate one bit! It was raining! "We still have four hours until the party," James's mom reminded him. James sat by the window and stared at the sky. After an hour, the rain slowed to a drizzle, and another hour later, it stopped. By the time of the party, the sun smiled down on the group, and James smiled, too!

KEY QUESTIONS

1. PERSONIFICATION ONE: Find an example of personification about bad weather.

2. PERSONIFICATION TWO: Find an example of personification about good weather.

3. CHALLENGE: Make up your own personification about rain and use it in a sentence.

4. CONTEXT CLUES: What do you think *anticipated* means?

☐ worried about
☐ cancelled
☐ looked forward to

5. S-T-R-E-T-C-H: Describe your dream birthday party. Be sure to use some personification in your writing.

The Ball Game

Shelly went to watch her hometown team play baseball. But now it was the bottom of the ninth inning, and the scoreboard told the sad story: Shelly's team was losing by one run. Her team was up at bat, but there were already two outs. She thought the day was sure to end in **defeat**. Before she knew it, though, the bases were loaded, and the team's star hitter, Juan Garcia, was up at the plate. Fortunately, Juan's bat knew just what to do. Swat! It was a grand slam! The scoreboard sang a new tune. Shelly's team had won!

KEY QUESTIONS

1. PERSONIFICATION ONE: Find an example of personification about the game's score.

2. PERSONIFICATION TWO: Find an example of personification about the last hit.

3. CHALLENGE: Find one more example of personification in the story.

4. CONTEXT CLUES: What do you think *defeat* means?

☐ loss
☐ happiness
☐ hunger

5. S-T-R-E-T-C-H: Describe your favorite sport, using at least three examples of personification.

Things Happen

Adam's mom had told him a million times not to throw balls in the house. But it was raining outside, and Buddy, their dog, really wanted to play fetch. Adam was extra careful throwing the ball, but even so, it knocked over his mom's favorite vase, shattering it. *Oh, no!* thought Adam, *Mom will never talk to me again!* But when his mom got home from work, she smiled from ear to ear. Her boss had told her she was doing a great job and had given her a big **raise**. Adam nervously told her about the vase, but she just grinned and said, "It's okay. These things happen."

KEY QUESTIONS

1. HYPERBOLE ONE: Find an example of hyperbole about playing inside.

2. HYPERBOLE TWO: Find an example of hyperbole about how Adam thinks his mom will react.

3. CHALLENGE: Find another example of hyperbole about his mother's expression.

4. CONTEXT CLUES: What do you think *raise* means?

☐ increase in pay ☐ big smile
☐ nice vase

5. S-T-R-E-T-C-H: Adam's mom responded differently than he expected. Why do you think she didn't get mad?

A Truly Terrible, Ginormous Smoothie Disaster

Friends Brad and Holly were at the mall's food court. Suddenly, Holly got a text from Brad: "Please come to the smoothie stand, **pronto**. I'm having a truly terrible, frightful problem!" Holly texted back: "What's wrong?" Brad responded: "Hurry! This is one of the most ginormous disasters EVER!" So Holly rushed to the smoothie stand. "What's wrong?" she repeated, when she found her friend. "They're out of strawberry smoothies," said Brad. "Well, you like blueberry," said Holly. "Just order a blueberry smoothie." Brad broke into a big smile. "I knew you could help," he said. "You're the best friend in the whole history of the world!"

KEY QUESTIONS

1. HYPERBOLE ONE: Find Brad's first hyperbole.

2. HYPERBOLE TWO: Find Brad's second hyperbole.

3. CHALLENGE: Find another example of hyperbole in the story.

4. CONTEXT CLUES: What do you think *pronto* means?

☐ slowly ☐ smoothly ☐ quickly

5. S-T-R-E-T-C-H: Hyperboles are great for exaggerating small problems. Imagine you spilled a glass of water. Describe the situation in a paragraph, using lots of hyperboles.

Skate Away

On his birthday, Malcolm planned to get the thing he wanted more than anything in the whole universe—a new skateboard. His birthday was on the last day of July, and all month long he watched the calendar, waiting for the day to arrive. It took forever! Finally the big day came. Malcolm and his mom went skateboard shopping. He didn't want to **browse**. He knew just the one he wanted. It had a cool, blue design and a smooth, easy ride. When they came out of the shop, Malcolm hopped on the board. "See you at home," he said to his mom, and happily skated off.

KEY QUESTIONS

1. HYPERBOLE ONE: Find an example of hyperbole about Malcolm's wish for a skateboard.

2. HYPERBOLE TWO: Find an example of hyperbole about time moving slowly.

3. CHALLENGE: Write a sentence that uses the hyperbole *took forever*.

4. CONTEXT CLUES: What do you think *browse* means?

☐ go skateboarding
☐ go home
☐ look around

5. S-T-R-E-T-C-H: Write about something that you thought you wanted "more than anything in the whole world."

An Amazing, Exciting, Incredible Invention!

Imagine a stack of your homework papers sitting on your desk. A breeze blows through an open window. Oh, no! Suddenly, all your papers go flying. You scurry around trying to gather them up. But they end up scattered to the four corners of the world. You wind up getting an F on the assignment. Don't let this sad situation **befall** you! For a limited time, we are offering the most amazing, exciting, incredible invention ever! Are you curious? Do you wonder what this life-changing item might be? Yes, indeed, folks, we're talking about a paperweight. Hurry and get yours while supplies last.

KEY QUESTIONS

1. HYPERBOLE ONE: Find an example of hyperbole related to papers getting blown by the breeze.

2. HYPERBOLE TWO: Find an example of hyperbole related to an invention.

3. CHALLENGE: Fill in the blanks with three more examples of hyperbole. The most _____, _____, _____ invention ever!

4. CONTEXT CLUES: What do you think *befall* means?

☐ forget about　☐ happen to
☐ make cry

5. S-T-R-E-T-C-H: Advertisements are full of hyperboles. Dream up something to sell, and then write an advertisement for it that's full of hyperboles.

Not My Best Day

Last week, as Van was walking to school, it started pouring. He didn't have an umbrella, and when he got to school Van was **soaked**.  "Just a little rain outside," he said to his teacher. A while later, he started to sneeze. He sneezed for five minutes straight. "Just a few sneezes," Van told the school nurse. Before long, his throat felt sore, and his muscles began to ache. "You have the flu," the nurse said. She called Van's mom, who came and picked him up. As they walked to the car, Van tripped, fell in a puddle, and ripped his pants. "This isn't my best day," Van said.

KEY QUESTIONS

1. UNDERSTATEMENT ONE: Find an example of understatement about the weather.

2. UNDERSTATEMENT TWO: Find an example of understatement about how Van feels.

3. CHALLENGE: Find one more example of understatement in the story.

4. CONTEXT CLUES: What do you think *soaked* means?

☐ very sick
☐ very tired
☐ very wet

5. S-T-R-E-T-C-H: Have you ever had a day when everything went wrong? Write about it.

Rena's Robot

It was Rena's turn to show off the robot she'd made. It could do 100 different things. Rena was excited, but she wanted to keep her cool. Using the controller, she made the robot move in various directions. It did all the moves perfectly. "It can follow a few commands," she said. Next, she directed the robot to lift a pitcher of water and pour it into a glass without spilling a single drop. The audience was dazzled. "That went OK," said Rena. After that, the judge walked over and studied the robot. "Not bad, not bad at all," he said. Then he made an announcement. "First place goes to the maker of this absolutely **superb** robot."

KEY QUESTIONS

1. UNDERSTATEMENT ONE: Find an example of understatement used by Rena.

2. UNDERSTATEMENT TWO: Find another example of understatement used by Rena.

3. CHALLENGE: Find an example of understatement used by the judge.

4. CONTEXT CLUES: What do you think *superb* means?

☐ excellent ☐ okay ☐ awful

5. S-T-R-E-T-C-H: Write a paragraph in which you describe something you're very proud of, but play it cool with understatement.

Cowboy Tex

Lin and her family were on a one-week camping **excursion**. Their guide, Tex, was a genuine cowboy. On the first day, they got to ride horses. As Lin's horse crossed a ditch, she was rocked back and forth and nearly fell. "It might get a tiny bit bumpy," said Tex. Later, as they were setting up their tents, they got caught in a terrible rainstorm. "Looks like you got a teeny bit wet," said Tex. That night, the weather cleared. Sitting near the campfire, Lin was amazed by how huge the sky looked. It seemed like there were a billion stars. "Yup, I can count a couple stars up there," said Tex with a wink.

KEY QUESTIONS

1. UNDERSTATEMENT ONE: Find an example of understatement related to horseback riding.

2. UNDERSTATEMENT TWO: Find an example of understatement related to weather.

3. CHALLENGE: Find another example of understatement in the story.

4. CONTEXT CLUES: What do you think *excursion* means?

☐ trip ☐ tent ☐ type of writing

5. S-T-R-E-T-C-H: Cowboy Tex is good at understatement. Write a mini-play starring Tex in which he uses three instances of understatement.

To the Top

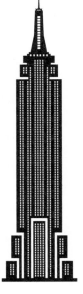

Carlos and his family were visiting New York City. They had plans to go to the top of the Empire State Building—102 floors up! There was only one problem: Carlos was terrified of heights. "It IS a little high up," he said, nervously. His mom offered to take Carlos shopping while his dad and sister went to the top. But Carlos wanted to **conquer** his fear, so he bravely went along. He felt proud standing with his family at the top of the skyscraper as they looked out on the whole huge city. "The view's not too shabby," he said, with a grin.

KEY QUESTIONS

1. UNDERSTATEMENT ONE: Find an example of understatement about the height of the Empire State Building.

2. UNDERSTATEMENT TWO: Find an example of understatement about the view.

3. CHALLENGE: Write a sentence about something exciting that contains an example of understatement.

4. CONTEXT CLUES: What do you think *conquer* means?

☐ climb ☐ overcome ☐ laugh at

5. S-T-R-E-T-C-H: Have you ever overcome a fear? Write about it.

Babysitting Fun

Daria was stuck babysitting her little brother, Davey. "This is going to be fun," she said, with a frown. First, Davey wanted to play a board game. Soon, he grew frustrated and knocked over the pieces. "You're such a great sport," sighed Daria. Next, he **donned** the superhero costume he'd worn a month ago for Halloween. He raced around shouting, carrying the plastic pumpkin he'd used to collect candy. "Wanna see what's in my pumpkin?" asked Davey. "I'm sure it's totally amazing," said Daria, flatly. Davey showed her. It was still filled with Halloween candy! "You can have whatever you want," he said. Now, that really WAS amazing!

KEY QUESTIONS

1. IRONY ONE: Find something ironic that Daria says about babysitting.

2. IRONY TWO: Find something ironic that Daria says about playing a game.

3. CHALLENGE: Find another ironic thing that Daria says.

4. CONTEXT CLUES: What do you think *donned* means?

- [ ] flew
- [ ] wore
- [ ] cleaned

5. S-T-R-E-T-C-H: What happens next in this story? Write a sequel in which Daria says three or more ironic things to her brother, Davey.

Trash Talking

Jack and Clyde played basketball one-on-one. The first to score 20 points would be the winner. Jack was a quiet kid. Clyde liked to talk a lot. Jack took a shot and missed. "Nice one," said Clyde. When Jack missed again, Clyde said: "Hey, you're a real superstar." Jack may have missed some shots, but he also made quite a few. Meanwhile, Clyde mostly talked trash. Soon, Jack led, 18–10. He made another basket, winning the game. That's when Clyde fell silent at last. That's also when Jack finally spoke up. "You've gotten very talkative, Clyde," he said, with a **sly** smile. "I wonder why?"

KEY QUESTIONS

1. IRONY ONE: Find something ironic that Clyde says to Jack.

2. IRONY TWO: Find something else ironic that Clyde says to Jack.

3. CHALLENGE: Find something ironic that Jack says to Clyde.

4. CONTEXT CLUES: What do you think *sly* means?

- [ ] clever
- [ ] happy
- [ ] big

5. S-T-R-E-T-C-H: Clyde was a poor sport during his game with Jack. What lesson does he learn? Write about it.

Running Late

Maura rode the bus to a job interview. She read a library book called *Never Be Late*. The book 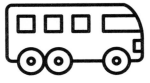 was overdue. The book offered tips on being **punctual**. The week before, Maura had been 30 minutes late for a job interview. When she finally arrived, the interviewer said, "Thanks for being on time!" She didn't get the job. Maura hoped this book would help her stop being late. The book was so interesting that she didn't pay attention and she missed her stop. Now she would be late for her interview. "Gee, this book is REALLY helpful!" Maura said to herself.

KEY QUESTIONS

1. IRONY ONE: Find an example of irony at Maura's first job interview.

2. IRONY TWO: Find an example of irony when Maura is on the bus.

3. CHALLENGE: Find one more example of irony in the story. Hint: It has to do with the library book.

4. CONTEXT CLUES: What do you think *punctual* means?

- ☐ on time
- ☐ smart
- ☐ a new job

5. S-T-R-E-T-C-H: Have you ever been late for something? What happened? If you've never been late, how do you manage to be so punctual? Write about it!

Eating Brussels Sprouts

Troy liked spinach. He also liked broccoli and green beans. But he **thoroughly** hated brussels sprouts. When his mom put down his plate for dinner and he saw three brussels sprouts next to the chicken and rice, he was not very happy. "Oh boy, my favorite," he said to his mom, with a frown. Then he had an idea. His sister loved brussels sprouts. He offered them to her. "It's hard to give them up," Troy said, "but I will, since you're such a nice sister." His mom overheard this and said that eating three brussels sprouts wouldn't kill him. He ate all three and survived.

KEY QUESTIONS

1. IRONY ONE: Find an example of irony when Troy is talking with his mom.

2. IRONY TWO: Find an example of irony when Troy talks with his sister.

3. CHALLENGE: Use the ironic phrase "Oh, boy, my favorite" in referring to something you don't like.

4. CONTEXT CLUES: What do you think *thoroughly* means?

- ☐ totally
- ☐ hardly
- ☐ officially

5. S-T-R-E-T-C-H: Write a paragraph about a food you *love* eating.

A Walk in the Woods

Mandy visited her cousin Ella, who lived in the mountains. They went for a walk in the woods, and Mandy listened to the sweet sound of birds: *tweet, tweet.* "Keep an eye out for snakes," Ella said. Mandy **halted** in her tracks. "*Snakes?*" Ella said not to worry: "We probably won't see any." But the very next minute, Mandy thought she heard one: *rattle, rattle.* Fortunately, it was just some leaves. Then she thought she heard a snake going *hissssssss!* But it was only an insect in the grass. "Are you having fun?" Ella asked. "Not really," Mandy said. "Let's go back to your house and ride bikes!"

KEY QUESTIONS

1. ONOMATOPOEIA ONE: Find an example of onomatopoeia that sounds like a snake.

2. ONOMATOPOEIA TWO: Find another example of onomatopoeia that sounds like a snake.

3. CHALLENGE: Find a third example of onomatopoeia in this story.

4. CONTEXT CLUES: What do you think *halted* means?

- ☐ ran
- ☐ listened
- ☐ stopped

5. S-T-R-E-T-C-H: Write a short paragraph that uses at least two examples of onomatopoeia that you know or make up yourself.

Peace and Quiet

Tyrell tried to study for his test, but he couldn't concentrate. There was a fly in his room. It went *buzz, buzz* around his head. Tyrell got up and opened the window, and after a few minutes, the fly flew outside. *Ah*, Tyrell thought. *Peace.* A minute later, the cat came in and started to *meow, meow* loudly by his feet. "No, Fluffy. Not now! I have a test tomorrow!" The cat scratched her head a few times and then **sauntered** out of the room. Then someone started honking a horn. *Honk, honk, honk! What next?* Tyrell thought. Thankfully, a moment later it stopped, and all that was left was silence!

KEY QUESTIONS

1. ONOMATOPOEIA ONE: Find an example of onomatopoeia that sounds like an insect.

2. ONOMATOPOEIA TWO: Find an example of onomatopoeia that sounds like a pet.

3. CHALLENGE: Find another example of onomatopoeia in this story.

4. CONTEXT CLUES: What do you think *sauntered* means?

- ☐ walked leisurely
- ☐ stretched
- ☐ flew

5. S-T-R-E-T-C-H: What does a jackhammer sound like? How would you write it?

Triple-Chocolate Peanut Delights

Keisha was selling cookies to raise money for her school. If she could sell 10 more boxes, she'd win a gift card to the amusement park. But it wasn't going too well. Everyone kept saying no. She pressed the doorbell at the latest house. *Ding-dong!* A **cantankerous**-looking woman answered. "What do you want?" she scowled. Keisha was tempted to just walk away. Instead she said: "I'm selling triple-chocolate peanut delights." The woman's face brightened. "*Yum, yum!* Those are my favorites. I'll take 10 boxes." What a surprise! Keisha won the trip! On her way home, she shouted: "*Yippee!*"

KEY QUESTIONS

1. ONOMATOPOEIA ONE: Find an example of onomatopoeia that relates to sound.

2. ONOMATOPOEIA TWO: Find an example of onomatopoeia that relates to taste.

3. CHALLENGE: Find another example of onomatopoeia in the story.

4. CONTEXT CLUES: What do you think *cantankerous* means?

☐ lonely ☐ sweet ☐ cranky

5. S-T-R-E-T-C-H: Many examples of onomatopoeia feature two slightly different words, such as *ding-dong* or *jingle-jangle*. Can you think of some more? Make a list!

The Crackling, Clicking, Clanking Calculator

For the science fair, Ari made a calculator. It was the size of a shoebox. There were bells and lights and wires sticking out everywhere. His teacher, Ms. Griffin, tapped *10 x 10* onto the keyboard. The calculator was **clamorous**. First it made a little *click, click, click.* Then the sound got louder. It went *CLANK, CLANK CLANK!* Then, the calculator buzzed and rattled and hiccupped. Finally, a piece of paper popped out. It read: "100." Miss Griffin said: "Congratulations, Ari. Your calculator gave the correct answer, 100. That will also be your grade for your science fair project."

KEY QUESTIONS

1. ONOMATOPOEIA ONE: Find an example of onomatopoeia related to a quiet sound.

2. ONOMATOPOEIA TWO: Find an example of onomatopoeia related to a loud sound.

3. CHALLENGE: This passage is filled with examples of onomatopoeia. Find five more.

4. CONTEXT CLUES: What do you think *clamorous* means?

☐ joyful ☐ noisy ☐ quiet

5. S-T-R-E-T-C-H: Machines make lots of sounds. Dream up a machine and use at least three examples of onomatopoeia to describe the sounds it makes.

Super-Silly Sis

My super-silly sister Sarah likes to **imitate** everything I do. When I put my poofy, permed hair in a pretty ponytail, she does it, too, because she wants to look just like me. She copies the way I dress and the music I like. When I got braces on my teeth, she twisted up some foil and put it in her mouth. "I can't wait to get braces, too!" she said. My mom said Sarah just looks up to me and wants to be my best buddy. I guess there are worse problems to have!

KEY QUESTIONS

1. ALLITERATION ONE: Find an example of alliteration that uses the letter *s*.

2. ALLITERATION TWO: Find an example of alliteration that uses the letter *p*.

3. CHALLENGE: Write a sentence that contains an example of alliteration with the letter *s*.

4. CONTEXT CLUES: What do you think *imitate* means?

☐ answer
☐ copy
☐ criticize

5. S-T-R-E-T-C-H: What does the narrator mean when she says, "There are worse problems to have"? Explain.

Awesome Amigos

When Rob started at a new school, he became friends with a boy named Diego. One day, Diego invited Rob to come over after school. Rob was shocked to find that at home, Diego and his parents spoke Spanish! "Wow, that's so cool," Rob said. He had no idea that Diego was **bilingual**.

"My parents were born in Puerto Rico," Diego explained. "But they want to make sure my brother and I have sensational Spanish-speaking skills, so we practice it at home." Diego spoke Spanish perfectly, but his English was totally tip-top, too! Diego told Rob they were now "amigos"—Spanish for "friends."

¿Cómo estás?

Bien.

KEY QUESTIONS

1. ALLITERATION ONE: Find an example of alliteration that uses the letter *s*.

2. ALLITERATION TWO: Find an example of alliteration that uses the letter *t*.

3. CHALLENGE: Write a sentence that contains an example of alliteration with the letter *t*.

4. CONTEXT CLUES: What do you think *bilingual* means?

☐ able to speak two languages
☐ able to speak English
☐ able to make friends easily

5. S-T-R-E-T-C-H: Write about a friend who can do something you think is cool. Use two examples of alliteration.

FIGURATIVE LANGUAGE: ALLITERATION

A Burger of Beef

Max went with his parents to dinner at a fine restaurant. Everything on the menu had a fancy name. One menu choice, for example, was "A tuna and tofu taco with tomatoes." There was also "Sizzling snails in savory sauce with a side of succotash." Nothing on the menu sounded **remotely** good to Max. Soon, the waiter arrived to take Max's order. "What would the young gentleman like?" asked the waiter. "Can I just get a hamburger?" asked Max. "Yes, indeed," said the waiter. "I will arrange for the kitchen to make a burger of beef inside a baked brown bun."

KEY QUESTIONS

1. ALLITERATION ONE: Find an example of alliteration that uses the letter *t*.

2. ALLITERATION TWO: Find an example of alliteration that uses the letter *s*.

3. CHALLENGE: Find another example of alliteration in this story.

4. CONTEXT CLUES: What do you think *remotely* means?

- ☐ laughably
- ☐ even slightly
- ☐ extremely

5. S-T-R-E-T-C-H: Even this passage's title uses alliteration. Dream up a title for a new story that uses alliteration.

FIGURATIVE LANGUAGE: ALLITERATION

Bonnie's Brand-New Bike

Bonnie's brand-new bike sat waiting in front of her house. It was white with wire wheels. Bonnie hopped on and went for her very first ride. She set off down the street. She turned into the nearby woods. She powered down pathways and pedaled through puddles. *Splish, splash!* She **maneuvered** the bike through the mud and the muck. After an hour, Bonnie rode home and parked in the same spot. It was no longer a white bike. In fact, it was caked and covered in crumbly dirt. Bonnie's bike didn't look brand-new anymore. But it was fast and fabulously fun to ride!

KEY QUESTIONS

1. ALLITERATION ONE: Find an example of alliteration that uses the letter *p*.

2. ALLITERATION TWO: Find an example of alliteration that uses the letter *m*.

3. CHALLENGE: This story is filled with alliteration. Find three more examples.

4. CONTEXT CLUES: What do you think *maneuvered* means?

- ☐ dragged
- ☐ skillfully moved
- ☐ threw

5. S-T-R-E-T-C-H: Using alliteration, write a story about a messy adventure.

IDIOMS

Saturday Chores (Card 1)
1. *Blew a gasket* means "got mad."
2. *Disaster area* means "mess."
3. Answers will vary.
4. *Mound* means "a small mountain."
5. Answers will vary.

The Tortoise and the Hare (Card 2)
1. *Piece of cake* means "easy."
2. *Like a bolt out of the blue* means "suddenly."
3. Another idiom is *slow as molasses.*
4. *Lumbering* means "slow and awkward."
5. Answers will vary.

A Dose of Laughs (Card 3)
1. *The apple of his eye* means "much loved."
2. *Laughter is the best medicine* means "laughter makes you feel better."
3. Answers will vary.
4. *Adored* means "loved."
5. Answers will vary.

First-Day Jitters (Card 4)
1. *Break the ice* means "put people at ease."
2. *You can't judge a book by its cover* means "something may be different than it first appears."
3. Answers will vary.
4. *Anxious* means "worried."
5. Answers will vary.

Besties! (Card 5)
1. *A night owl* means "someone who stays up late."
2. *An early bird* means "someone who gets up early."
3. Answers will vary.
4. *Numerous* means "many."
5. The idiom is *on the other hand.* Sentences will vary.

When Pigs Fly (Card 6)
1. *When pigs fly* means "never."
2. *Call it a day* means "give up."
3. *Barrels of fun* is another idiom in the story.
4. *Taunting* means "teasing."
5. Answers will vary.

A Blessing in Disguise (Card 7)
1. *Bent out of shape* means "upset."
2. *Blessing in disguise* means "good thing that seems bad at first."
3. Answers will vary.
4. *Engrossed* means "deeply interested."
5. Answers will vary.

Sick Day (Card 8)
1. *Under the weather* means "ill."
2. *Back on your feet* means "feel better."
3. *under the weather*
4. *Blurted* means "said suddenly."
5. Answers will vary.

Up and Up (Card 9)

1. *As cool as a cucumber* means "calm."
2. *Butterflies in his stomach* means "a nervous feeling."
3. Answers will vary.
4. *Trepidatious* means "fearful."
5. Answers will vary.

Superpowers (Card 10)

1. *Hanging out* means "spending time together."
2. *In a snap* means "quickly."
3. Answers will vary.
4. *Relive* means "do again."
5. Answers will vary.

It's Not Rocket Science (Card 11)

1. *Take it easy* means "relax."
2. *It's not rocket science* means "it's easy."
3. Answers will vary.
4. *Standard* means "usual."
5. Answers will vary.

Bad Hair Day (Card 12)

1. *Went overboard* means "did too much."
2. *Silver lining* means "good thing."
3. Answers will vary.
4. *Gaped* means "stared open-mouthed."
5. Lisa's mom says it because Lisa's hair is now so short that it won't make her head hot.

Let It Snow! (Card 13)

1. *On cloud nine* means "very happy."
2. *Took the wind out of his sails* means "disappointed him."
3. Answers will vary.
4. *Forecasting* means "predicting."
5. *He threw on his clothes* is an idiom about getting dressed.

Summer of Wonder (Card 14)

1. *Wish list* means "a list of things you want to do."
2. *Branch out* means "try something new."
3. Answers will vary.
4. *Behold* means "see."
5. Answers will vary.

You Dream It, We Make It (Card 15)

1. *Pulling my leg* means "joking."
2. *Back to the drawing board* means "time to start over."
3. Answers will vary.
4. *Baffled* means "confused."
5. Answers will vary.

Wally's Wallet (Card 16)

1. *In hot water* means "in trouble."
2. *A wild-goose chase* means "hopeless search."
3. Answers will vary.
4. *Inspected* means "carefully looked at."
5. Answers will vary.

Surprise, Surprise! (Card 17)

1. *Spilled the beans* means "told the secret."
2. *Clammed up* means "fell silent."
3. Answers will vary.
4. *Reveal* means "make known."
5. Answers will vary.

Up in the Attic (Card 18)

1. *Music to her ears* means "good news."
2. *A trip down memory lane* means "a time to remember the past."
3. Answers will vary.
4. *Rummaged* means "searched."
5. Answers will vary.

"You Can Say That Again" (Card 19)
1. *Break a leg* means "good luck."
2. *Pull yourself together* means "control your emotions."
3. *You can say that again* means "I agree with you."
4. *Bizarre* means "very strange."
5. Answers will vary.

Yo-Yo Expert (Card 20)
1. *Adding insult to injury* means "making a bad situation worse."
2. *Cut corners* means "do things quickly and badly."
3. *As proud as a peacock* is another idiom in the story.
4. *Instructional* means "teaching."
5. Answers will vary.

Same Old Juan (Card 21)
1. *Down in the dumps* means "sad."
2. *Same old* means "same as before."
3. Answers will vary.
4. *Apprehensive* means "worried."
5. Answers will vary.

Super Sight (Card 22)
1. *Clear as day* means "very clear."
2. *Do the trick* means "fix the problem."
3. Answers will vary.
4. *Sporting* means "wearing."
5. *Nina wasn't crazy about getting glasses* is another idiom.

Missing Mate (Card 23)
1. *No big deal* means "not a problem."
2. *Spick-and-span* means "very clean."
3. Answers will vary.
4. *Reunited* means "brought back together."
5. Answers will vary.

Where's Duke? (Card 24)
1. *Brokenhearted* means "very sad."
2. *A sight for sore eyes* means "something happy to see."
3. Answers will vary.
4. *Gleefully* means "happily."
5. Answers will vary.

Math Magic (Card 25)
1. *Achilles' heel* means "weakness."
2. *Put his nose to the grindstone* means "work hard."
3. Answers will vary.
4. *Perplexing* means "hard to understand."
5. Answers will vary.

Lights Out (Card 26)
1. *Hit the hay* means "went to bed."
2. *Sleeping like a log* means "sound asleep."
3. Answers will vary.
4. *Arduous* means "difficult."
5. Answers will vary.

Smart Umbrella (Card 27)
1. *Raining cats and dogs* means "raining hard."
2. *Greatest thing since sliced bread* means "best ever."
3. Answers will vary.
4. *Retrieves* means "gets."
5. Answers will vary.

Capture the Flag (Card 28)
1. *I'm all ears* means "I'm listening closely."
2. *As easy as ABC* means "super easy."
3. Answers will vary.
4. *Diversion* means "thing that redirects attention."
5. Answers will vary.

Diving Bee (Card 29)

1. *Having second thoughts* means "doubting."
2. *A stroke of luck* means "a good occurrence."
3. *A stroke of luck* completes the sentence.
4. *Petrified* means "so frightened one can't move."
5. Answers will vary.

Scratchy Sweater (Card 30)

1. *Like two peas in a pod* means "very close."
2. *The last straw* means "the final bad thing."
3. Answers will vary.
4. *Devious* means "sly."
5. Answers will vary.

SIMILES

Haircut Day (Card 31)

1. A simile about having messy hair is *as big as a bush.*
2. A simile about being thin is *as skinny as a string bean.*
3. Answers will vary.
4. *Shorn* means "cut off."
5. Answers will vary.

The Big, Bad, Poorly Informed Wolf (Card 32)

1. A simile related to a storm is *like a raging hurricane.*
2. A simile related to something that's well-built is *as strong as steel.*
3. Another simile in the story is *like a billowing smokestack.*
4. *Exhausted* means "very tired."
5. Answers will vary.

Sweet and Tart (Card 33)

1. A simile that means excited is *as impatient as a puppy.*
2. A simile about a strong taste is *as sour as a lemon.*
3. Another simile in the story is *as pretty as a picture.*
4. *Tart* means "sour."
5. Answers will vary.

A Ferocious Beast (Card 34)

1. A simile related to fire is *like a pair of flickering flames.*
2. A simile related to sewing is *teeth as sharp as needles.*
3. A simile about a wild animal is *like a ferocious beast.*
4. *Pounce on* means "suddenly attack."
5. Answers will vary.

The Itsy-Bitsy Spider (Card 35)

1. A simile about Sal's legs is *like tough metal clamps.*
2. A simile about droplets of water is *as shiny as jewels.*
3. Answers will vary.
4. *Drenched* means "very wet."
5. Answers will vary.

A Green Breakfast (Card 36)

1. A simile that means you have a big appetite is *as hungry as a lion.*
2. A simile that mentions something you see outdoors is *as green as grass.*
3. Answers will vary.
4. *Beaming* means "smiling."
5. Answers will vary.

The Kite (Card 37)

1. A simile related to a color is *as yellow as the sun*.
2. A simile about how something moves is *like a dancer in the sky.*
3. Answers will vary.
4. *Ideal* means "perfect."
5. Answers will vary.

Nuts for Winter (Card 38)

1. A simile about the landscape in winter is *as bare as an empty cupboard.*
2. A simile that describes the weather is *as icy as a freezer.*
3. Answers will vary.
4. *An abundance* means "a large amount."
5. Answers will vary.

All Fixed! (Card 39)

1. A simile about being special is *like a treasure.*
2. A simile about the way Anika treated the old doll is *like a tiny bird.*
3. Answers will vary.
4. *Fragile* means "breakable."
5. Answers will vary.

Fresh Cookies! (Card 40)

1. A simile that mentions an animal is *as fast as a cheetah.*
2. A simile related to an eye is *as quick as a wink.*
3. Answers will vary.
4. *Aroma* means "nice smell."
5. Answers will vary.

Frog Prince (Not) (Card 41)

1. A simile about eyes is *eyes as green as emeralds.*
2. A simile about hair is *like spun gold.*
3. Answers will vary.
4. *Perusing* means "reading carefully."
5. Answers will vary.

The Flimflam Man (Card 42)

1. A simile related to an animal is *as happy as a bunny with a carrot.*
2. A simile related to entertainment is *like the crowd at a circus.*
3. Answers will vary.
4. *Flimflam* means "tricky."
5. Answers will vary.

The Rescue (Card 43)

1. A simile about being sweet and thoughtful is *as kind as an angel.*
2. A simile about being intelligent is *as wise as an owl.*
3. Another simile in the story is *as fast as the wind.*
4. *Injured* means "hurt."
5. Answers will vary.

Shy Student (Card 44)

1. A simile about a movement is *shook like leaves in the wind.*
2. A simile about how someone sounds is *as smooth as silk.*
3. Answers will vary.
4. *Quiver* means "shake."
5. Answers will vary.

A Surprise at the Zoo (Card 45)

1. A simile about not moving is *as still as statues.*
2. A simile about following closely is *like a shadow.*
3. *As big as a house* is another simile in the story.
4. *Glimpse* means "look."
5. Answers will vary.

A Skating Lesson (Card 46)

1. A simile about something being smooth is *like a sea of polished glass*.
2. A simile about something happening fast is *as quick as a lightning strike.*
3. Another simile in the story is *clung to the wall like a sticker.*
4. *Sprawled* means "lying awkwardly."
5. Answers will vary.

Human Bowling (Card 47)

1. A simile about the acrobats in white tights is *like a set of bowling pins.*
2. A simile about the acrobat dressed in black is *like a rolling bowling ball.*
3. *As loud as thunder* is another simile in the story.
4. *Hurtled* means "moved at great speed."
5. Answers will vary.

A Day at the Beach (Card 48)

1. A simile related to a color is *as red as a lobster.*
2. A simile related to the ocean is *as warm as a bath.*
3. Another simile in the story is *like a field of tiny, sparkling diamonds.*
4. *Elated* means "thrilled."
5. Answers will vary.

Ant Feast (Card 49)

1. A simile about two strong ants is *like a pair of tiny bodybuilders.*
2. A simile about a delicious meal is *like a big, tasty Thanksgiving feast.*
3. Another simile in the story is *like a cozy cottage.*
4. *Gnawed* means "chewed."
5. Answers will vary.

Salty Treat (Card 50)

1. A simile about a dry mouth is *as dry as a desert.*
2. A simile about a sweet flavor is *like a little sugary explosion*.
3. Another simile in the story is *like fast-changing weather*.
4. *Scrumptious* means "delicious."
5. Answers will vary.

METAPHORS

S'mores Time (Card 51)

1. A metaphor about something round in the sky is *the full moon was a big hunk of tasty yellow cheese.*
2. A metaphor about things that twinkle in the sky is *the stars were little sparkly, sugar-dusted gumdrops.*
3. A metaphor related to Elle's father is *his words were soothing music to Elle's very hungry tummy.*
4. *Emerged* means "came out."
5. Answers will vary.

City and Suburb (Card 52)

1. A metaphor about something small is *her bedroom is a shoebox.*
2. A metaphor about something large is *Violet's house is a castle.*
3. Answers will vary.
4. *Resides* means "lives."
5. Answers will vary.

My Robot, Rob (Card 53)

1. A metaphor related to being good at basketball is *he's a bounding kangaroo.*
2. A metaphor related to eating a lot is *Rob is a bottomless pit.*
3. Two more metaphors in the story are *he's a graceful gazelle* and *a shining star.*
4. *Bounding* means "leaping upward."
5. Answers will vary

Different Weather (Card 54)

1. A metaphor about bad weather is *the rain was a thick curtain of water.*
2. A metaphor about heat is *they walked into a giant oven.*
3. Answers will vary.
4. *Sweltering* means "very hot."
5. Answers will vary.

Kurt's Game (Card 55)

1. A metaphor that mentions something you wear is *basketball is a shoe that doesn't fit.*
2. A metaphor that mentions an animal is *Kurt is a fish in water.*
3. Answers will vary.
4. *Exceptional* means "excellent."
5. Answers will vary.

A Book of Poetry (Card 56)

1. A metaphor about a facial feature is *your eyes are two twinkling stars gracing the night sky.*
2. Another metaphor about Pam Poodle is *your fur is puffy clouds floating in the heavens.*
3. A metaphor that describes Hank is *you're a regular book of poetry.*
4. *Clutched* means "held tightly."
5. Answers will vary.

Beach Bliss (Card 57)

1. A metaphor for the wind is *the ocean breeze was a giant fan.*
2. A metaphor that tells how Ty views the beach is *the beach is a great big sandbox.*
3. Another metaphor about the beach is *the beach is my favorite library.*
4. *Scorching* means "very hot."
5. Answers will vary.

A Roller-Coaster Day (Card 58)

1. A metaphor about Jorge's winning shot is *he was king of the world!*
2. A metaphor about Jorge's entire day is *it was a real roller coaster.*
3. Answers will vary.
4. *Postponed* means "put off to a later date."
5. Answers will vary.

Night Chicken (Card 59)

1. A metaphor related to a mammal is *Ben was a real night bat.*
2. A metaphor about an object in the night sky is *the full moon was an enormous eyeball.*
3. A metaphor related to a bird is *Chad was a night chicken.*
4. *Scurried* means "hurried."
5. Answers will vary.

Visiting Granddad (Card 60)

1. A metaphor about Nora's visits with her granddad is *visits with him were trips in a time machine.*
2. A metaphor about the days of winter is *the days are a dark cave.*
3. Answers will vary.
4. *Regaled* means "entertained."
5. Answers will vary.

My Teenage Brother (Card 61)

1. A metaphor about eating cookies is *Matt was a giant vacuum.*
2. A metaphor about Matt's growth spurt is *He was a fast-growing beanstalk.*
3. Answers will vary.
4. *Surpassed* means "went beyond."
5. Answers will vary.

Harry the Hurricane (Card 62)

1. A metaphor about being shy is *he's a turtle in his shell.*
2. A metaphor about being speedy is *he was a fast-moving hurricane.*
3. Answers will vary.
4. *Timid* means "shy."
5. Answers will vary.

Amazing Colors (Card 63)

1. A metaphor related to something you look through is *the canyon walls were a colorful kaleidoscope.*
2. A metaphor related to a treat is *the sky above was pink cotton candy.*
3. Answers will vary.
4. *Gobsmacking* means "amazing."
5. Answers will vary.

Lost in a Book (Card 64)

1. A metaphor related to Ana's home is *Ana's home was a zoo!*
2. A metaphor related to reading is *Ana's book was a peaceful land that she could get lost in.*
3. Answers will vary.
4. *Tranquil* means "calm."
5. Answers will vary.

Princess Poppy Leaves the Castle (Card 65)

1. A metaphor about summer weather is *the sun is a warm, happy friend smiling down on you.*
2. A metaphor about fall weather is *the leaves are little ballerinas twirling in the air.*
3. A metaphor about winter weather is *the snowflakes are video game aliens coming down to Earth.* Answers will vary.
4. *Appealing* means "good and interesting."
5. Answers will vary.

Hot Sauce (Card 66)

1. A metaphor related to something found in a kitchen is *my mouth is an oven turned up to 400 degrees.*
2. A metaphor related to a natural disaster is *my mouth is a volcano blowing its top.*
3. Drop the word *like* to turn the sentence into a metaphor: "They were panting dogs with their tongues hanging out."
4. *Unbearably* means "not able to be tolerated."
5. Answers will vary.

Who's There? (Card 67)

1. A metaphor that describes something comfortable is *the bed was a soft, fluffy cloud.*
2. A metaphor about the weather is *the wind was a howling wolf.*
3. Answers will vary.
4. *Enervated* means "out of energy."
5. Answers will vary.

A Graceful Swan (Card 68)

1. A metaphor about Lucy's sister is *she's a graceful swan gliding across the stage.*
2. A metaphor about the people watching is *the audience was a symphony of clapping hands.*
3. Answers will vary.
4. *Standout* means "especially good one."
5. Answers will vary.

Moira and Melvin at the Movies (Card 69)

1. A metaphor involving a musical instrument is *Moira's laugh was a tinkling piano floating on a summer breeze.*
2. A metaphor involving a wild animal is *Melvin's laugh was a hyena that had eaten too much sugar.*
3. Melvin's laugh is *HAR! HAR! HAR!* It's clear because he has the loud laugh that sounds like a hyena.
4. *Raucous* means "loud and wild."
5. Answers will vary.

Johnny Flower Seed (Card 70)

1. A metaphor about Johnny is *Johnny was a nonstop spinning top.*
2. A metaphor related to flowers is *the backyard was a colorful painting come to life.*
3. Answers will vary.
4. *Whirled* means "spun round and round."
5. Answers will vary.

PERSONIFICATION

Opportunity Knocks (Card 71)

1. An example of personification related to a chance to do something is *opportunity was knocking.*
2. An example of personification related to a sound is *the vacuum hummed.*
3. Another example of personification in the story is *soon the floor was so clean that it beamed.*
4. *Strewn* means "scattered."
5. Answers will vary.

No Time for Boredom (Card 72)

1. An example of personification about something in the yard is *a tall tree standing guard.*
2. An example of personification about something in the sky is *the stars winking overhead.*
3. Answers will vary.
4. *Gazed* means "looked."
5. Answers will vary.

Yard Sale (Card 73)

1. An example of personification about books is *the mystery novels were calling to him.*
2. An example of personification about a piece of furniture is *an old chair that groaned.*
3. Two more examples of personifications are *they put up a huge sign that screamed "Bargains!"* and *the glove lived on Jake's hand the rest of the summer!*
4. *Arbitrary* means "random."
5. Answers will vary.

A Boring Summer (Card 74)

1. An example of personification related to summer is *the days had slowly strolled by.*
2. An example of personification related to writing is *soon, her pencil raced across her paper.*
3. Another example of personification is *the bike had been her loyal friend.*
4. *Humdrum* means "boring."
5. Answers will vary.

Mister Goofball to the Rescue (Card 75)

1. An example of personification related to something you see during a storm is *the lightning leaped across the sky.*
2. An example of personification related to something you hear during a storm is *the thunder grumbled.*
3. This sentence includes two examples of personification: "The angry storm kept raging."
4. *Distract* means "amuse."
5. Answers will vary.

The Big Trip (Card 76)

1. An example of personification related to the car Vivian is in is *the car sighed as it came to a stop.*
2. An example of personification related to the other cars on the highway is *soon the cars began their march down the highway again.*
3. Answers will vary.
4. *Shrieked* means "screamed."
5. Answers will vary.

Snorg's Halloween (Card 77)

1. An example of personification related to the sun is *the sun slipped below the horizon to sleep for the night.*
2. An example of personification related to the moon is *the moon gazed down.*
3. Another example of personification in the story is *the doorbell screamed.*
4. *Doled out* means "handed out."
5. Answers will vary.

Banana Bungle (Card 78)

1. An example of personification related to a camera is *the camera loves you.*
2. An example of personification related to a fruit is *that banana peel hates me.*
3. Answers will vary.
4. *Romantic* means "in love."
5. Answers will vary.

Watching the Weather (Card 79)

1. An example of personification about bad weather is *the weather didn't cooperate one bit!*
2. An example of personification about good weather is *the sun smiled down on the group.*
3. Answers will vary.
4. *Anticipated* means "looked forward to."
5. Answers will vary.

The Ball Game (Card 80)

1. An example of personification about the game's score is *the scoreboard told the sad story.*
2. An example of personification about the last hit is *Juan's bat knew just what to do.*
3. Another example of personification is *the scoreboard sang a new tune.*
4. *Defeat* means "loss."
5. Answers will vary.

HYPERBOLE

Things Happen (Card 81)

1. An example of hyperbole about playing inside is *a million times.*
2. An example of hyperbole about how Adam thinks his mom will react is *Mom will never talk to me again!*
3. Another example of hyperbole about his mom's expression is *she smiled from ear to ear.*
4. *Raise* means "increase in pay."
5. Answers will vary but might include: *She doesn't get mad because she's in a good mood after getting a raise at work.*

A Truly Terrible, Ginormous Smoothie Disaster (Card 82)

1. Brad's first hyperbole is *I'm having a truly terrible, frightful problem!*
2. Brad's second hyperbole is *This is one of the most ginormous disasters EVER!*
3. Another example of hyperbole in the story is *You're the best friend in the whole history of the world!*
4. *Pronto* means "quickly."
5. Answers will vary.

Skate Away (Card 83)

1. An example of hyperbole about Malcolm's wish for a skateboard is *the thing he wanted more than anything in the whole universe.*
2. An example of hyperbole about time moving slowly is *it took forever.*
3. Answers will vary.
4. *Browse* means "look around."
5. Answers will vary.

An Amazing, Exciting, Incredible Invention! (Card 84)

1. An example of hyperbole related to papers getting blown by the breeze is *scattered to the four corners of the world.*
2. An example of hyperbole related to an invention is *the most amazing, exciting, incredible invention ever!*
3. Answers will vary.
4. *Befall* means "happen to."
5. Answers will vary.

UNDERSTATEMENT

Not My Best Day (Card 85)

1. An example of understatement about the weather is *just a little rain outside.*
2. An example of understatement about how Van feels is *this isn't my best day.*
3. Another example of understatement is *just a few sneezes.*
4. *Soaked* means "very wet."
5. Answers will vary.

Rena's Robot (Card 86)

1. An example of understatement used by Rena is *it can follow a few commands.*
2. Another example of understatement used by Rena is *that went OK.*
3. An example of understatement used by the judge is *not bad, not bad at all.*
4. *Superb* means "excellent."
5. Answers will vary.

Cowboy Tex (Card 87)

1. An example of understatement related to horseback riding is *it might get a tiny bit bumpy.*
2. An example of understatement related to weather is *looks like you got a teeny bit wet.*
3. Another example of understatement is *Yup, I can count a couple stars up there.*
4. *Excursion* means "trip."
5. Answers may vary.

To the Top (Card 88)

1. An example of understatement about the height of the Empire State Building is *it IS a little high up.*
2. An example of understatement about the view is *the view's not too shabby.*
3. Answers will vary.
4. *Conquer* means "overcome."
5. Answers will vary.

IRONY

Babysitting Fun (Card 89)

1. Something ironic Daria says about babysitting is *"This is going to be fun."*
2. Something ironic Daria says about playing a game is *"You're such a great sport."*
3. Another ironic thing that Daria says is *"I'm sure it's totally amazing."*
4. *Donned* means "wore."
5. Answers will vary.

Trash Talking (Card 90)

1. Something ironic that Clyde says to Jack is *"Nice one."*
2. Another ironic thing that Clyde says to Jack is *"Hey, you're a real superstar."*
3. Something ironic that Jack says to Clyde is *"You've gotten very talkative."*
4. *Sly* means "clever."
5. Answers will vary.

Running Late (Card 91)

1. An example of irony at Maura's first job interview is *"Thanks for being on time!"*
2. An example of irony when Maura is on the bus is *"Gee, this book is REALLY helpful!"*
3. Another example of irony is *the book was overdue.*
4. *Punctual* means "on time."
5. Answers will vary.

Eating Brussels Sprouts (Card 92)

1. An example of irony when Troy is talking with his mom is *"Oh boy, my favorite."*
2. An example of irony when Troy talks with his sister is *"It's hard to give them up."*
3. Answers will vary.
4. *Thoroughly* means "totally."
5. Answers will vary.

ONOMATOPOEIA

A Walk in the Woods (Card 93)

1. An example of onomatopoeia that sounds like a snake is *rattle, rattle.*
2. Another example of onomatopoeia that sounds like a snake is *hissssss!*
3. A third example of onomatopoeia in the story is *tweet, tweet.*
4. *Halted* means "stopped."
5. Answers will vary.

Peace and Quiet (Card 94)

1. An example of onomatopoeia that sounds like an insect is *buzz, buzz.*
2. An example of onomatopoeia that sounds like a cat is *meow, meow.*
3. Another example of onomatopoeia in the story is *Honk, honk, honk.*
4. *Sauntered* means "walked leisurely."
5. Answers will vary.

Triple-Chocolate Peanut Delights (Card 95)

1. An example of onomatopoeia that relates to sound is *Ding-dong!*
2. An example of onomatopoeia that relates to taste is *Yum, yum!*
3. Another example of onomatopoeia in the story is *Yippee!*
4. *Cantankerous* means "cranky."
5. Answers will vary.

The Crackling, Clicking, Clanking Calculator (Card 96)

1. An example of onomatopoeia related to a quiet sound is *click, click, click.*
2. An example of onomatopoeia related to a loud sound is *CLANK, CLANK, CLANK!*
3. Five more examples of onomatopoeia are *tapped, buzzed, rattled, hiccupped,* and *popped.*
4. *Clamorous* means "noisy."
5. Answers will vary.

ALLITERATION

Super-Silly Sis (Card 97)

1. An example of alliteration that uses the letter *s* is *super-silly sister Sarah.*
2. An example of alliteration that uses the letter *p* is *put my poofy, permed hair in a pretty ponytail.*
3. Answers will vary.
4. *Imitate* means "copy."
5. Answers will vary.

Awesome Amigos (Card 98)

1. An example of alliteration that uses the letter *s* is *sensational Spanish-speaking skills.*
2. An example of alliteration that uses the letter *t* is *totally tip-top, too.*
3. Answers will vary.
4. *Bilingual* means "able to speak two languages."
5. Answers will vary.

A Burger of Beef (Card 99)

1. An example of alliteration that uses the letter *t* is *a tuna and tofu taco with tomatoes.*
2. An example of alliteration that uses the letter *s* is *sizzling snails in savory sauce with a side of succotash.*
3. Another example of alliteration in the story is *a burger of beef inside a baked brown bun.*
4. *Remotely* means "even slightly."
5. Answers will vary.

Bonnie's Brand-New Bike (Card 100)

1. An example of alliteration that uses the letter *p* is *she powered down pathways and pedaled through puddles.*
2. An example of alliteration that uses the letter *m* is *she maneuvered the bike through the mud and the muck.*
3. Three more examples of alliteration in the story are *Bonnie's brand-new bike, white with wire wheels,* and *caked and covered in crumbly dirt.*
4. *Maneuvered* means "skillfully moved."
5. Answers may vary.